sex180

Other books by Chip Ingram

God: As He Longs for You to See Him
Holy Ambition: What It Takes to Make a Difference for God
*Holy Transformation: What It Takes for God to Make a Difference
   in You*
I Am with You Always: Experiencing God in Times of Need
*Love, Sex, and Lasting Relationships: God's Prescription for
   Enhancing Your Love Life*

sex180
the next revolution

chip ingram
and tim walker

BakerBooks

Grand Rapids, Michigan

Published by Baker Books
a division of Baker Publishing Group
P.O. Box 6287, Grand Rapids, MI 49516-6287
www.bakerbooks.com

Published in association with Yates & Yates, LLP, Attorneys and Counselors, Orange, California.

Printed in the United States of America

Library of Congress Cataloging-in-Publication Data
Walker, Tim, 1968
    Sex 180 : the next revolution / Chip Ingram and Tim Walker.
        p.   cm.
    Includes bibliographical references.
    ISBN 0-8010-4529-0 (pbk.)
    1. Sex—Religious aspects—Christianity. 2. Teenagers—Conduct of life. I. Ingram, Chip, 1954– . II. title. III. title: Sex one hundred eighty.
    BT708.W35 2005
    241'.66—dc22   2005018709

To Annie and all her friends for living out sex180 in the most amazing and authentic way I've ever seen.
—Chip Ingram

To Jennifer: Your love and the love of Christ that flows through you amazes me.
—Tim Walker

contents

acknowledgments

[From Chip]

To Tim Walker: Thank you for taking up the mantle to get this truth into the lives of teens. It has been a privilege working with you on this project.

To Vicki Crumpton and the Baker team: Thank you, Vicki, for seeing the potential of this project to help teens. You and the Baker team took the initiative to make a good idea a reality.

To Walk Thru the Bible: Thank you all for your support and encouragement all along the way.

[From Tim]

To God: For reminding me every step of the way that I need you—not for words or time or anything else—I just need you.

To Chip Ingram: Thanks for giving me the opportunity of a lifetime and entrusting to me a message so close to your heart. It has infiltrated my heart as well, and I find that I'm a lot more revolutionary than I ever thought I was.

To Jennifer: I'm supposed to be a master of words, but somehow they just seem inadequate when I think of all you are to me. I love you very much. Thanks for walking on this journey with me. It's crazy. It's wonderful. It's scary. But I'm glad you're here every step of the way. Thank you for entrusting your life to me and allowing me to entrust my life to you.

To Grayson, Hamilton, and Bryce: You are my three favorite little superheroes in all the world. I'm so blessed to be your dad. I love all three of you very much.

To the revolutionaries for inspiring me and living this out— Annie, Bobby, Audrey, Bo, Mike, and Amy.

To Dad and Mom: For giving me a foundation so clear and so real that even though I strayed at times, I never went too far. Thanks also for providing a quiet place to write this book.

To my family, whose love for me has never wavered: You may not have known all the details of my life, but you always saw who I really am, even when I couldn't. Thank you, Marc, Donita, Cory, Sharon, Steve, Lynne, Stephanie, Steve B., Janet, Bob, Grandpa Olin, Grandma Cerny, Aunt Shorty, Charles, Martha, Hanyaw, MeMaw, (can you tell I'm from the South?), and my Walker/McCook/Ray/Olin/Cerny families.

To all my friends who prayed for me when I needed to know that what looked impossible to me wasn't to God and gave me much-needed encouragement along the way: Joey Smith, Lare and Amy McCreary, Joe and Anda Barnett, Mark and Gwen Brague, Don Munn, Chris Rogers, Jim and Laura Hunter, Mary Ledford, Buck and Pam Dyer, Laurin Makohon, Travis Stoneback, Jim Gabrielsen, Paula Kirk, Chris Tiegreen, the Walk Thru the Bible staff, the Next Exit Youth Group at Restoration Church of God, NXAM Sunday school, Fern Nichols and the Moms in Touch, Tim Brenner, Crystal Kirgiss, Jim Hancock, and Robert and Sarah Mullins.

To Vicki Crumpton, the Baker publishing team, and Curtis Yates: Thanks for walking me through the process of writing a book and for helping me communicate both my heart and God's.

And if I forgot anyone, I'm sorry. Maybe I'll get to write another book and can mention you then!

acknowledgments

1
disclaimer

You picked up this book because . . .

you wanted to know what in the world "sex180" means. We'll get to that in a minute.

you thought the cover looked better than the other books about sex (yep, Tim totally judges a book by its cover too).

you liked the word *revolution*.

your mom/dad/grandma/youth pastor gave this book to you.

Whatever the reason, you've made it this far. You opened the book to this page. We'll definitely try to live up to your expectations for the rest of the book. (By the way, we're really impressed that you're reading the introduction.)

But before we start, you need to know a few things.

First, who are we? We have a confession. We're both married guys—with kids. Yeah, we know. We may have just lost some cred with you. After all, we're married. We have sex. And we're dads, so you might be thinking we have some kind of ulterior motive or that your parents asked us to write this book. BTW, they didn't.

The truth is, we've both made some mistakes along the way when it came to sex. This book isn't penance. And we're not expecting you to be perfect. But if we had both seen God's heart behind what he says about sex earlier in our lives, we would have made some different choices. We might have ended up with a few less scars.

We've seen up close what happens when we think about sex completely on the outside—when it's all about what we can and can't do—and totally miss God's heart and plan. We've also seen how the wrong view of sex can mess up a lot of other people's lives too.

And we're not off the hook here. It's just as important for adults to understand what God thinks about sex as it is for students. It doesn't take much looking to see proof of that in our culture—or maybe you see proof in your own family.

We live in the same world you live in. We have to click the remote, delete the emails, and try to remind ourselves that what God says about sex isn't what we hear and see every day.

But we don't have to deal with rainbow parties, friends with benefits, "are you hot" websites, and all the other junk you deal with.

Our generations have really messed up the world for yours. We don't want you to make the same mistakes—or worse. We believe there's a better way to think about and do sex—God's way.

We know who you are. One thing that draws people to what our culture says about sex is the fact that it seems to acknowledge something most Christians ignore: we're sexual. It's part of how God made each one of us. God made sex. He created it to bring two people together in a binding way that is both mysterious and awesome. To ignore the fact that you have desires and are curious about sex is about as real as reality TV. We believe God made those desires a part of each one of us, and we want to get to the heart of why he did. Then we

sex180

can better understand what it means to explore and live out that part of our lives in a way that is both honoring to him and beneficial for us.

One-word answers don't cut it anymore. We definitely want to give props to organizations and people who have worked hard over the years to get students to start thinking about sex in a way that's different than what our culture has been feeding us. They've done a great job of challenging people to talk about sex when most people preferred to remain mute. They've shown people what it means to connect your beliefs to your sexuality. They've even shown teenagers who want to wait that there are a lot of teens out there who are just like them. But the reality is that some teens with pledge cards and promise rings are having sex. "No" and "wait" just aren't good enough anymore—we want to know why. Sex isn't just about what you do or don't do.

New math. We're not offering a formula—"Follow this plan and you'll live happily ever after." Life doesn't work that way. Neither does faith. It's not about following all the external rules. It's about getting face-to-face with God, so close that you see his heart. There'll be advice in this book. We'll tell you stories of people who are living out a sex180. But the truth is, you've got to own this stuff. You've got to understand it on a whole new level. The church answers aren't going to cut it when you want to be so close to your boyfriend or girlfriend that skin-on-skin seems like the natural next move. But you're never going to own it until you understand why God says what he says about sex and you begin to see his heart behind his words.

Sex180 T-shirts, bumper stickers, necklaces, tattoos—not going to happen. This isn't a fashion revolution. This isn't a trend or marketing campaign. Revolutions aren't about bracelets and rings. Revolutions aren't about rallies. Revolutions are about people who are passionate about something, so passionate that it affects the way they think, feel, and act. Then it affects those around them. Revolutions start in the heart, then move outward.

Are you ready to find out more?

13

disclaimer

sex180

So what is sex180?

Well, here's what it's not:

>**IT'S NOT** another T-shirt wearing, jewelry-clad movement.
>
>**IT'S NOT** another ad-slogan response to real-life desires.
>
>**IT'S NOT** another big stadium rally about abstinence.
>
>**IT'S MORE** than no.
>
>**IT'S MORE** than wait.

Sex180 is a new position on sex and sexuality. This is a book about sex. Not a how-to or how-not-to book—that's all been done.

This is a book for people who realize that sexuality is part of their makeup but are over the way our culture, including Christian culture, talks about it.

This is a book for people who realize that something's wrong, deep-down core wrong, with the way we think, believe, and act in regard to sex.

Sex180 is for people who want something different—drastically different. A full 180 degrees different. It's for people who want a revolution—a second sexual revolution—to happen with them, their friends, their family, their school, and their world.

It's time. Because the way things are now . . . well, they're not so great.

[the truth about sex]

In a survey conducted by NBC News and *People* magazine[1] in early 2005, the vast majority (87%) of the teens ages 13 to 16 participating in the survey said that they had not had sexual intercourse.

That's good news, right? Well, it is until you read more stats from the survey.

Thirty-seven percent of 15- to 16-year-olds said they had touched someone's genitals or private parts. Nineteen percent had had oral sex. Forty percent of that group said that they had had oral sex to avoid sexual intercourse.

Do the math. Many people may not be going all the way, but they sure are getting close.

Many people may not be going all the way, but they sure are getting close.

In the same survey, the students who had not been sexually intimate at all said they had made that decision because they believe they are too young (75%). Others fear the potential consequences: pregnancy (74%), STDs (71%), parents' reaction (65%). Given the right circumstances and situations, each of these reasons could easily have an expiration date.

Sixty-six percent of the teens in the survey said, "Waiting to have sex is a nice idea, but no one really does." And if they do wait, they aren't waiting for very long. An American Psychological Society study found that 60% of college students who had pledged virginity during

sex180

reasons people wait to have sex

- waiting to be more emotionally mature
- waiting because of religious beliefs
- consider it a self-respect issue
- waiting until the "right time"
- afraid that it might change future goals and plans

their middle school or high school years had broken their vow to remain abstinent until marriage.[2]

Author and *Washington Times* editor Julia Duin tells of a time when she was lecturing a college freshman class on sexuality and was surprised by some of the feedback she got from students during a time of discussion about abstinence and virginity.

"A few of these freshmen may have been part of a 'True Love Waits' campaign or had their parents give them a 'promise ring' along with the reminder not to sleep around until marriage, but the other 90 percent hadn't heard much in the way of gripping reasons for staying chaste."[3]

So why would someone who had made a vow or pledge break their "promise"? Why would someone not wait?

[expiration date]

For some people, the wait just gets too long. The average age of marriage for guys is 27 and 25 for girls. If all you're doing is waiting, you will probably come to a point when you're going to get tired of it.

Some people stop waiting because they find love. They want to get closer to this person who makes them feel all these wonderful things inside. They want to do some type of action that shows the other person just how much they care about him

sex180

or her, so they're willing to break their promise to God. Maybe they never even saw it as a promise to God in the first place but more of a promise to the future spouse. And if you think you've found Mr. or Mrs. Right, isn't that good enough?

Monica, a freshman at Truman State University, confesses that religion used to be her reason for waiting to have sex, but now that she's away from home, that reason doesn't seem to be as important.

"It's just something that's so special, and I want to save it for someone who's special," Monica said. "I don't know about [waiting] until marriage, but waiting for someone special."[4]

[the right one]

In the *People* magazine/NBC News poll, meeting the right person was the top reason people had sex before marriage. But how do you know when you've found the right person? Many people have found the "right one," crossed the physical boundaries, and realized in the afterglow of sex that the perfect relationship wasn't so perfect.

In their book *Relationships*, Drs. Les and Leslie Parrott tell the story of Mike and Lauren, two college students whose story is echoed in a lot of relationships.

Lauren and Mike spent hours studying together, talking, and staring at each other—oblivious to the rest of the world. They thought they had the perfect relationship, and several months into it, they thought they were ready for what they believed was the natural next step.

They arrived late one night at Mike's apartment. Mike's roommate was gone, and Lauren started picking up on the signals that none of this was random. Mike was ready.

Mike began kissing Lauren passionately, whispering about her beauty and his intense desire to know all of her. He repeatedly declared his love and said he wanted them to show

sex180

each other how much love they shared. He clearly had an agenda.

Lauren told the Parrotts about the confusion going on inside her: "Mike believed in me, when no one else would. . . . I wasn't planning on having sex that night, but I knew that the future of our relationship would probably be over if we weren't intimate soon." During the next several months, Lauren became consumed with Mike. "He was all that mattered," as she put it. Sex soon became a part of all their dates. But when Lauren began talking about changing her summer plans to be with Mike, his passion quickly cooled. It was no real surprise that Lauren and Mike broke up before the end of the spring semester.[5]

[curiosity kills]

Curiosity is huge for some people. They just want to know what it's like to be desired by someone not just for your mind or personality but for your physical body. Plus, they want to move beyond all the textbook, biology class stuff. They don't want to just know about sex; they want to *know* about sex.

Curiosity was my (Tim's) main motivation. I'm the kind of guy who wants to know what's going on. I was the fun little kid who asked all the questions and gave his parents a dull, throbbing headache. I would eavesdrop on my parents' conversations, soaking up all the latest news. I wanted to know who was doing what and why they were doing what they were doing.

Part of that is how God wired me. It's a good trait to have—especially as a writer. But it can also be a bad thing. I wasn't just content to listen to "the talk" (you know, that awkward moment when your parents tell you about sex) and then park it, waiting for "that special day" when I got married. I wanted to know ahead of time what sex was all about. So when I found

sex180

a porn magazine, it fed my curiosity. The pictures in there weren't in my biology book. And that was just the beginning. Curiosity is seldom satisfied. The pictures made me want to know what those things felt like. So when an opportunity arose, I followed curiosity's lead.

[worried about your skills]

Some people are terrified they're not going to be good at sex. What if there's something weird or different about their body? What if they can't have sex? What if they wait all that time until after they're married and they don't like it? This motivates some people to put in some practice time. They're afraid they might get to the honeymoon and wonder, "So what are we supposed to do?"

Kay, age 16, wrote in to *YouthWalk* magazine (which Tim co-writes and edits):

> Most of my friends who are Christians have had many boyfriends and some have even slept with them. I was telling one of my friends that besides getting STDs or pregnant, it's best to wait until marriage. She snapped back that if you wait until you're married it will be really awkward for both of you and you'll be bad at it. She also said that if you wait till marriage, you'll always wonder if you're doing it right.

Think about this one. Sex isn't that complicated. You're going to know what to do. You're going to figure out what goes where. This isn't something you have to be good at. This isn't a skill you need to pick up. And why are you even worried about that? It's not like you're being graded!

When two people get married, they start out on a lifelong journey. They learn about each other. They go through all kinds of life experiences together. And part of that experience is learning about sex together. It's an adventure. It's something

sex180

for the two of you to explore together. And aren't adventures so much more interesting when you both are in a place you've never been before? Nobody said we have to be great at sex at first. But when it's in the context of a married relationship, you have plenty of opportunities to get better at it.

The reason some married couples don't have great sex in marriage is that it wasn't sacred to them before the wedding. There was no mystery. Maybe partner number 12 didn't match up to the porn they saw, or they find out sex is nothing like the romance novels or movies. They believed all the phony lies fed to them about love and sex, and now their expectations are completely distorted.

[happily ever after may never come]

Yeah, you might be thinking, *but what's the point in waiting for marriage when most marriages don't last that long anyway? What if I spend all this time holding out for this ideal goal when my future spouse might not do the same—or we both do, but then we become a divorce statistic?*

Susanna, a 17-year-old high school senior from Michigan, confesses, "You get to the point where you think there is no such thing as a real relationship anymore—that it's just something our moms and dads had."[6]

Lasting relationships are built on much more than just sex. Sex is part of it, but it takes a lot more than just sex to keep a marriage going. And if sex is your sole focus, you're missing the big picture of how awesome marriage can really be.

[the good and bad of desire]

According to that *People* magazine/NBC News poll we mentioned earlier, 34% of students who had sexual intercourse for the first time did so solely because they just wanted to have sex. They followed desire's lead. Some people give up waiting because they just don't feel like they can fight their desires anymore.

Desire is a normal, natural thing.

But desire is a normal, natural thing. When we follow our desires, they can motivate us to do good things. Psalm 40:8 says, "I desire to do your will, O my God; your law is within my heart." Proverbs 8:11 states that wisdom is precious and "nothing you desire can compare with her."

But desire can also lead us to do things that will ultimately hurt us. Check out what writers Jim Hancock and Kara Eckmann Powell say about desire:

> Desire is good. Except when it's bad.
>
> Think about it. Desires drive one person to sacrifice herself in pursuit of a cure for AIDS.
>
> Desire drives another person to indulge in behavior that spreads HIV.
>
> Desire is tricky that way.
>
> Healthy desire generates commitment and propels accomplishment.
>
> Unhealthy desire, on the other hand (and there's always that other hand), fuels lust.
>
> And lust, as the book of James says, gives birth to sin—which, when it's full-grown, gives birth to death.[7]

[it's not so bad]

The way some people within the church talk about sex, you may think that if you have sex before you're married, it's going to be a horrible experience. You're going to hate every minute of it, and nothing will be pleasurable about it.

Here's the truth: if you have sex before marriage, you may actually enjoy it. You may find yourself surprised how much it stirs up something within you, and you'll probably want to do it again.

But at some point, you're going to get burned. You may continue to get pleasure from having sex, but sooner or later all the unseen entanglements—the emotional and the spiritual—are going to come into play. And you're going to find yourself either being used or using someone. You're going to find yourself on the receiving end of a brutal breakup. What once felt so great physically is now going to hurt so bad emotionally.

[the "who to do" list]

If you're feeding on the media a little too much, you may find yourself viewing sex as just something to get out of the way. An item to check off your "to do" list (or maybe it should be "who to do" list), a rite of passage toward adulthood.

Let's eavesdrop on a counseling session between counselor Paula Reinhart and a 20-year-old woman. Think of it as reality TV—very sad, messed-up reality TV. The 20-year-old woman's current boyfriend is insensitive and her divorced dad has married a woman she can't stand. She is sleeping with her boyfriend and has a sexual history. Recounting her experiences, she eventually mentions the loss of her virginity.

Here's the truth: if you have sex before marriage, you may actually enjoy it. But at some point, you're going to get burned.

"I didn't want to have a bad experience in losing my virginity—like some of my friends," she says. "So I found a guy I knew but didn't feel anything special for, and I had sex with him. That way I could just get it over with."

Paula Reinhart responded, "Your virginity was something you wanted to 'just get over'?"

"Well, sure. That way I would enjoy sex more with guys I really cared about."[8]

Is that all sex is—just something to get over? What about when you're married someday—what's that conversation going to be like? Do you really think your future spouse is going to be impressed by your ability to have sex with someone you said you cared nothing about? Come on, what are we training for here, people? Is that the best thing you have to bring to the table in a relationship?

[taken away]

For some people, it's not a matter of whether they chose to have sex. The choice was made for them in a violent way, either through rape or abuse. The reality of a fallen, sinful, and overly sexual world has wreaked havoc in their lives. The sin of another person has taken something very precious away from them. They never had a say in the matter.

Some people choose to deal with that tragedy by just growing numb to their sexuality and letting any boundaries they may have had previously go away. "After sex has been taken instead of given," says Jenny, who was raped by a guy in her neighborhood as a teenager, "it's like you are already tainted. So what difference does it make anymore? It's not like I could offer purity to my husband anyway."

That may be how Jenny saw herself, but it wasn't how God saw her. That wasn't how he intended for Jenny to lose her virginity. It was stolen from her by the evil, sinful choice of another person. And while Jenny bought into the lie she was "damaged goods," God always wanted to restore to Jenny what had been violently taken away.

[the Bible doesn't ever say so]

You're not going to find that one verse that says word for word, "Thou shalt not have sex till you're married" or "Here's a specific list of what you can and can't do on a date." But that doesn't mean the Bible has nothing to say about sex. In both the Old Testament and the New Testament, the Bible ad-

sex180

dresses things that would make even the sleaziest talk show host blush. It includes stories about rape, incest, and adultery. Plus, the Bible does give us some clear-cut boundaries that are vital when it comes to sex:

> It is God's will that you should be sanctified: that you should avoid sexual immorality; that each of you should learn to control his own body in a way that is holy and honorable, not in passionate lust like the heathen, who do not know God; and that in this matter no one should wrong his brother or take advantage of him.
>
> 1 Thessalonians 4:3–6

> Among you there must not be even a hint of sexual immorality, or of any kind of impurity, or of greed, because these are improper for God's holy people. Nor should there be obscenity, foolish talk or coarse joking, which are out of place.
>
> Ephesians 5:3–4

If you're hung up on the fact that the Bible doesn't give specific, detailed info about your particular question, you may not be looking hard enough. Or you could just be looking for some kind of green light to justify doing what you want to do.

It's like a little kid who asks her mom, "Can I play ball in the street?" The mom says no. Ten minutes later, the mom hears a car slam on its brakes and sees the little girl playing in the street. The mom asks, "Why?"

The response from the little girl? "I wasn't playing ball. I was jumping rope. You said I couldn't play ball in the street." The little girl knew she shouldn't play in the street. So she decided she was going to manipulate the situation to get what she wanted. She got it. But she also put herself in danger.

We love the Bible. We believe the Bible is God's truth speaking to our hearts (even though we might not always want to hear what it says). And as you read, you're going to see that

God has a lot to say about sex and sexuality. While the Bible may not address issues like oral sex or Internet porn directly, it sure does communicate God's truth in a way that can help you figure it out. Sometimes you just have to be honest enough with yourself to make the connection.

[clueless]

When it comes to sex, some people think the Bible is out of touch with how our modern world views sex. They think it's outdated. But actually many of those long-ago cultures were just as sex-crazy as ours—if not more. Especially the cities of Corinth, Rome, Ephesus, Galatia, and all the other churches Paul wrote to in the New Testament. Most of them would make MTV's Spring Break specials look tame.

Check out what was going on there, according to writer Jim Hancock:

> Those folks lived in cultures in which male and female prostitution was a part of religious life (so just imagine life among the pagans). They lived in towns where sacrificing girls was the main event at the shrine on the hill. They lived in cities where boys were sex objects for wealthy men. They lived in cultures where women were property—collected, traded, used, and discarded. And no one raised an eyebrow, let alone a helping hand.[9]

[so why should I wait?]

Let's get one thing straight: not having sex isn't only about avoiding pregnancy, STDs, or anything else. Those are all outside reasons. And honestly, sometimes even those big life-changing reasons are going to seem like a long shot, and you'll be willing to take the risk. You need an internal reason too.

sex180

Not having sex isn't just about avoiding intercourse. Plenty of people are getting physical with one another, touching each other, and doing things to one another that aren't actually sexual intercourse but sure are sexual. They're getting together in intimate ways and trying to pretend there's no intimacy or connection.

God wants you to wait. Not so you can be some statistic in an abstinence poll. Not so you can prove some political or social agenda wrong. He wants you to wait because when you don't, you get hurt. You get wounded. You get used. And you use others.

Not having sex isn't just about avoiding intercourse.

He wants you to wait because he cares about you. He is saying no to something you may very much want now because he knows that the now—this way, this time, this relationship—has a short-lived satisfaction and that's all. But the adventure of sex in a lifelong commitment is so much better.

But then again, you've heard most of this before. That's why we need to dig deeper. That's why we need a second sexual revolution.

over it!

Sex is everywhere.

Sex is on TV.

Sex is in movies.

Sex is in music.

Sex is on the Web.

Sex is in magazines.

Sex is in books.

Sex is in high schools.

Sex is in youth groups.

People are having sex.

People are reading about sex.

People are talking about sex.

People are watching others having sex.

People are reacting to sex.

People are thinking about sex.

Yet with all of that, some part of the sex story is still not being told. People are looking for all kinds of external ways to explore sexuality, but they are running in the wrong directions. Sex isn't just about what we do or don't do, nor is it about the visible consequences like pregnancy or STDs.

Sex is a heart issue, one that our culture has made purely physical. The only time the heart is mentioned is when we're trying to justify the physical ("Oh, but we're sooo in love . . .").

Are you over all of this? You're tired of what our culture says about sex. Sure, you think sex is a good idea. Sure, you want to have sex someday (you are human). But you want something different—180 degrees different.

You want a revolution—a second sexual revolution—to happen with you, your friends, your family, your school, your youth group, and your world.

We want that too. People are physically, emotionally, or spiritually dying—or all of the above—all over the world because they just don't get it.

Look at the AIDS epidemic in Africa. In 2004, AIDS caused the deaths of an estimated 3.1 million people, including 2.6 million adults and 510,000 children under 15. The epidemic has spread largely through a culture of promiscuity—primarily through infected husbands, who have been with prostitutes and then have sex with their wives. Women and girls make up the approximately 58% of those infected with HIV.[1] In confidential surveys by World Vision, 72% of South African pastors admitted to having had extramarital affairs, with an average of 3 to 4 partners each.[2]

Look at the number of people soliciting children for sex. There are approximately 100,000 illegal child porn sites online. Twenty percent of people under 18 have been solicited for sex in a chat room.[3] An estimated 10 million children are commercially sexually exploited worldwide—and the numbers are increasing.[4]

Look at the number of people addicted to Internet porn. Requests for porn on search engines averages about 25% of the

sex180

total daily requests.[5] Thirty-four percent of Christian women admitted to intentionally accessing Internet porn—some of them to find out what their husbands were looking at, others due to their own Internet porn addiction.[6]

We need something drastic to change. We need a revolution, a second sexual revolution.

Voices are screaming out for change everywhere you turn.

[we're not going to take it anymore]

Benjamin, age 17, posted the following message on the YouthWalk website:

> It seems that 90% of all secular music deals with love. But the ideas are often so false. Either you're hearing a country song that talks about cheating on your wife while you're "down in Mexico," or you're hearing a rap song about someone shooting his mother, raping a girl, or "making love" with his girlfriend. And those are just the extremes from what seems innocent at first to what is just flat-out wrong. We listen to so many songs like that, we don't even stop to think about what we're listening to and how that can affect our mind. It really frustrates me because it's so obvious.

Benjamin is only one voice. But he's not the only one who's sick of what our culture's been force-feeding us about sex and sexuality.

We listened to a group of students one night over delicious enchiladas and warm chocolate chip cookies. They each came from very different backgrounds.

Some were dating, some were in relationships, and some were not.

One had been a Christian since she was kid; the others had been following Christ for two, three, four years at the most.

over it!

Most of them were from non-Christian homes. One guy's mom is a Christian, and his dad's Jewish. One girl's parents are atheists. Another's family just goes to church on holidays. One guy started going to church around September 11, 2001, and has pursued God ever since.

They are seniors and sophomores. Their musical interests range from Relient K to Casting Crowns to David Crowder. Favorite movies range from *Save the Last Dance* to *The Rock* to *A Walk to Remember*. Favorite TV shows include *24*, *Extreme Makeover: Home Edition*, and *Oprah*.

With all of these differences, they had one thing in common: they're all sick and tired of what's going on with how people think about and do sex.

They aren't perfect. They each have their own struggles of living out what they believe is both God's perspective on sex and his heart behind it. They fight the internal battle daily. Yet each one of them believes there's a better way to think about sex, a way that's 180 degrees different than what they are seeing and hearing. They're over how sex has been defined and played out.

You'll hear from these students throughout this book. They inspire us. They're probably a lot like you. They want a sex180; they want a different way to view sex and sexuality. They're passionate about God, his Word, and living out his truth.

Read and listen to the rumblings of the next revolution.

[who or what do you think is having the biggest influence on how people think about sex?]

MIKE (AGE 18): I'd say the biggest influence is TV. It has a huge influence on what students wear, what students do, and how they relate to each other in different situations.

sex180

ANNIE (17): Just going to the grocery store and seeing the covers of the magazines is horrible. The cover models aren't just half-naked; sometimes they're completely naked. Guys too. And then the stuff on the covers isn't any better—things like "Ten ways to enhance your sex life."

AUDREY (17): I used to read those magazines when I was younger because my parents were like, "Oh, they're just teen magazines." They didn't even look through them. But they're bad. I was learning a lot about sex. I didn't realize it. I bought into the media lie that when you love someone, you have sex with them. When you think you're ready, that's when you have sex.

ANNIE: It's not just magazines or TV—it's our whole environment. If you're into fashion and go into the cool stores, there are pictures of naked people on the wall. Sex is even at school. We had this girl come into our school and do a concert promoting "don't do drugs." She was 16. Her shirt was up to here and her skirt was down to there. She was dancing with sexual kinds of moves. It's just like sex is everywhere you go.

AUDREY: At the beginning of the concert, they were asking us what our anti-drug was. I could just imagine her coming out and being like, "Sex, my anti-drug."

MIKE: The problem is that media and society say in order for you to be accepted, you have to look this way or dress this way. The only way you're going to actually make it and be successful is if you show a lot of skin.

[what does our culture say about relationships?]

AMY (15): People always talk about guys and porn, and how it's an unrealistic view of girls, but have you ever thought about

over it!

chick flicks? That makes things unrealistic too. It's kind of like girl porn. It alters your vision of the guy.

ANNIE: This is the perfect guy. This is what he'll look like.

AUDREY: After the movie, I'm like, "Oh, I want a boyfriend like that."

AMY: I'm a girl. I like watching chick flicks. But it makes me have unrealistic expectations of the opposite sex.

AUDREY: Why I would consider it porn for girls is because girls are so much more emotional and boys are so much more visual. So it just feeds you. The chick flicks feed us to be like, "Oh, that's how it happens. They deserve to be together." They have sex and we're glad.

[it's real easy to point that stuff out in the media, but what about real life? how do you see those kinds of influences played out in how people actually live out their sexuality?]

MIKE: I see a lot of high school girls invest so much of their time into how they can please their boyfriend and do all this other stuff. Many girls who said they were waiting and wanting to be pure are like, "He really wants me to do this. That's fine. I'll do it." It's such an emotional thing. So many times, girls go out and totally give themselves to guys—they have sex—and then the guy leaves. The girls get so attached to them, but the guys just move on to the next girl.

AMY: I have a friend whose relationships always start out great, and then they get torn apart. She gets so attached because she's been sexually active with them. We were talking one weekend, and she told me, "You don't know how awesome I think it is that you're not going to have sex until you're married. I wish I would have done that." She just became

sex180

a Christian a year ago. She knows it's wrong, but sex has been such a big part of her life for the past six years. She wishes she could stop but she says she can't. She doesn't know how to have a relationship without it.

AUDREY: For some people, sex is just so much of a struggle that they don't even fight it anymore. They give up and say that won't be an aspect of their faith. It'll just be a separate part of their lives. I know so many Christians who are sexually active and are like, "A sin is a sin and it's not that big of a deal." They don't realize that there's a reason God doesn't want us to have sex. There's so much damage that comes from sex. There's so much hurt and baggage.

MIKE: This guy said to me one day in class, "I'm not going to get married till I'm 40 because I don't want to make a commitment. I want to go out there and have sex with as many girls as I can." It's so sad to see all these people who have gone out and had sex with multiple partners. What happens next? What happens if you can't have sex anymore? What happens when you get HIV or an STD? Before, you were the sex champion. Wow, that's great. You've got that on your record. Now you are on death row. Where is your identity after that? This is what you have to look forward to, a life of emptiness? Is that what you base your life on? I hate the stereotypical guy, because that is the stereotypical guy—"How many girls can I have sex with before I'm married?" Everyone's saying you've got to experience life—get drunk, smoke weed, have sex with 20 girls at once. But once you've done all that stuff, can you seriously look back at yourself in the mirror and say, "I'm so proud. I'm so happy. I want to give myself a pat on the back. I have accomplished every single thing and I'm just Superman"?

[so if you believe something different, how do you live that out—especially when it seems like the culture is screaming another message so loudly?]

ANNIE: I think as mature believers in Christ, we need to develop convictions about [what we watch], and when you're with a group of people, role model it. If someone's asking you to watch something you know you shouldn't be watching, say, "You know what? Personally, for me, I think I'm going to skip out on watching that because of the convictions God has given me. Maybe you think it's okay for you to watch; you just have to really think it through. There are clear guidelines God sets up."

AUDREY: There's this kid in one of my classes who makes sexual jokes all the time. He looks at me and asks, "Do these jokes make you mad?" And I'm like, "Yeah. I really just don't appreciate it. You know where I stand, and I know you're doing that just to make me mad." He said, "Sorry." And I said, "I think a lot of what you say is funny—it's just not always funny to me."

MIKE: Every time I turn on the TV, there's always something about sex. It came to a point where I unplugged my TV. We all know what is too much for us, what we can't handle, what we can't do. I think even beyond that, we have to look at what we can't handle and take that back a few steps. In every situation, everyone needs to ask him- or herself two questions. First, is this going to benefit me in my relationship with God? Second, is this going to benefit me overall as a person? I looked at my situation, and TV was totally pushing me away from God. Before I got rid of the TV, I would sit there flipping through channels, thinking, "That's so bad. I can't believe how bad it is. I'm going to watch this and see how terrible it is so I can write a letter about how bad it is." It's funny how much we think we can hide from God's eyes.

sex180

It was totally consuming me. During that time, my relationship with God was nothing. It was going nowhere.

BOBBY (15): Life isn't lived to fullness without God. Everything isn't quite as fun as it could be, as good as it could be. The same thing applies with sex. You do it without God and what happens? It's not what you expected. I think so many times people spiral into relationships because they think it's going to be something great, but deep down they're still hurting. There's so much emotional stuff tied to sex, and you've got to just wait until God says you're ready. He said marriage is that time to give the spiritual and emotional and everything that's linked to sex, that he made it in his intricate plan.

AUDREY: A huge change. A change from the way people act, the way people think.

AMY: Change in society.

ANNIE: It's a change in your mind, how you think about things.

BO (16): We all want to change the world; that's basically what a revolution is. Going out, setting your heart, your whole everything to changing the world for the better. Getting as many people on your side as possible to help you change the world, to what God wants to be done in the world.

BOBBY: You have to stand up and be proud that you're going to abstain, that you have a reason. There are so many good kids out there who just don't know about not having sex before marriage. That's why Christians have to take a stand. If we want a new sexual revolution, we're going to have to stand up. We have to make a difference in this world. We can't just give in. We have to be bold. We can't just sit in the back of the church and call it quits. We've got to be out there. When your friends talk about sex, don't be afraid to say, "The reason I'm not doing it is because I have God." That's the reason you're waiting—so say it proudly. I struggle with it all the time. I told my friend that I'm not having sex before marriage because of God and what he's done in my life. He doesn't understand that, but I think he has a certain respect for it. And hopefully, one day he will get it.

AUDREY: People sit back and say, "I can't really do anything. I'm just one person." But if all of them would just act on what they believe, there would be a revolution.

MIKE: There's definitely a problem. People are so misguided in their relationships and also with the concept of sex and how it's being done. Sometimes it takes a few people with a whole lot of passion to step up to the plate, and a revolution is started by a few people. There's sacrifice when it comes to revolution; it's a hard process. If it wasn't hard, it wouldn't be a revolution. I think in the long run, any revolution fought is something that has to be well worth the struggle.

[the cost]

Maybe you are reading all this, nodding your head in agreement, and thinking, "That's a great idea, but there's no way you're going to change the world. Sex is just too much a part of our world. Besides, people should be free to make their own choices. If I choose not to have sex, why does anyone else need to know? A revolution seems a little extreme, doesn't it?"

It does sound like another Christian bandwagon—"Hey, everyone jump on board this issue. We're going to straighten everyone out!"

Well, that is, until you start counting the cost.

Whether you're a virgin or you've been sexually active in your past (and maybe are in the present), the way our culture views sex is costing you something. You just may not have always realized you were paying.

It costs you something when you walk down the halls of your school. It costs you something every time you go online. It costs you something every time you look in the mirror and wonder if you're attractive enough. It costs you something every time you listen to music, watch a movie, or turn on the TV.

Because of the way sex is now in our culture, you have to be on your guard all the time. You have to wonder if the person you're talking to in a chat room is really another teen or if it's an online predator hoping to have sex with you. You have to wonder if the movie you're wanting to see is going to fill your head with some graphic scenes that really aren't that key to the plot. You have to wonder if the song that you enjoy on the radio, the one with that beat that just stays in your head, really is worth listening to.

Maybe it has cost you your family. Your dad or mom found someone new and left. You've seen your brother or sister get used time and time again because they give their hearts and their bodies freely away to anyone who seems to care.

You pay a price daily. You pay with your innocence, your pain, your heartache, or your regret.

We're not going to let this cost us anything else. We are not going to pay this price anymore.

We want a revolution!

Revolution means war—but instead of taking on people, we're fighting lies. Lies that are entrenched in our culture. Lies that so many people have bought into. Lies that make people think they've found what they've always been looking for—when the reality is, what they are settling for is so inferior to the real thing.

That's right, you've been played.

Are you sick of being fed lies about sex? Are you tired of all the ways sex is being played out both in the media and in people's lives?

Are you tired of being played as a pawn in a culture that thinks sex is just a game? That's right, you've been played. Duped. You've been led to believe that your sexuality is nothing more than a marketing technique—something to sell everything from chicken sandwiches to CDs to jeans to cars.

You've had sex crammed down your throat everywhere you turn. You've been sold a pack of lies that ruin lives and relationships, all while feeding someone else's bank account.

People think they own you.

They think they can manipulate you.

They think they can feed you whatever they want, and you'll buy it.

Are you sick of it?

Are you over it?

Then fight back.

Let's get this revolution started!

who, me?

4

Oh, yeah! Woo hoo! Change the world. Let's do it! Uh . . . how do you do that?

Revolution is a big word. (We know, there are bigger words, like *triskaidekaphobia*.) But we believe you can handle big words and make big changes. *Can we really change the world?* you might be thinking. *Who knows how to do that anyway?*

Oh, sure, some part of you thinks maybe you can—the dreamer in you wanting to believe that you can be a worldwide catalyst for change. Maybe it's the same part of you that thinks you can outwit everyone on *Survivor* or try out for *American Idol* and not be one of those people from the audition shows who can't sing.

But come on. How can you start a revolution when most of the people at your school don't even know you exist?

You can do this—and you don't have to have amazing communication skills or the kind of personality that pulls people to you. You just have to really believe what God says about sex and live out what you're talking about.

Revolutions never start big—they always start small. And revolutions have happened before. Think history class: the

Industrial Revolution, the American Revolution, the French Revolution.

Oh, yeah, and there was the first sexual revolution.

[the first sexual revolution]

In the 1960s, a handful of people looked at their culture and saw a lot of hypocrisy. They believed there was a better way to live in this world. They were sincere, and they were passionate.

Revolutions never start big.

They made signs like "Make Love, Not War." They showed the people in power that they were going to do something different. They openly challenged the established values, thinking, and manipulation of their lives. They preached a more open, expressive view of life in general, particularly sexuality. They made themselves and their views visible on college campuses. They rallied anywhere their voices would be heard. The end result was a cultural and sexual revolution.

In the 40 years from then until now, our culture has done a spin that has changed the course of the world. The first revolutionaries modeled their message in their lives and proclaimed it through their music and their art.

Everything shifted because a handful of people, mostly teens and young adults, believed something strongly enough and passionately enough to risk their lives and their futures for it. The first sexual revolution changed music. It changed literature. It changed media. It changed books. It changed economics.

The '60s did have something powerful and good about them. Even though our current culture is a mess as a result, the first revolutionaries sincerely wanted to make a difference. They were willing to take on the establishment and the status quo. They didn't just say words—they lived out what they believed.

sex180

According to an author and theologian named Francis Schaeffer, those revolutionaries diagnosed the problem with the culture accurately, but their solution didn't work. They were sincere about the values they advocated, but we've since seen how those values haven't worked out that well.

[wasn't that great?]

Ever since that first sexual revolution, a lot of people have been talking about and having sex. So how's that working out for them? Not so well.

We can watch people do wild things to each other on the movie screen, on TV, or on our computer monitors that we would never think about watching in person.

We can cheer a couple on as they finally have sex, even though each person is already married, because the story line leads us to believe that now they've found true love.

We can dance around to catchy tunes with great beats but lyrics that talk about treating one another as personal sex toys.

We can gyrate around one another, simulating sex with our clothes on, thinking we're just dancing when inside we know there's a lot more getting started than just the party.

We can show as much skin as possible and think it makes us more confident and powerful.

We can engage in sex and say that it is purely a physical act—no emotions involved.

We can use people for experience, personal pleasure, or entertainment.

Man, things are good, aren't they?

Yes, those "sexual pioneers" and the generations that have followed have left quite a mess for your generation. In our efforts to be so "forward" and avoid any semblance of rewinding to those "good old days" (which, when you really start digging around, weren't exactly heaven on earth either), we have

who, me?

tolerated a bunch of stuff that was once considered way out of line and created a culture that is constantly trying to outdo itself in fear of being so repressed again.

When we say 180, we don't mean we want to go back to the time before the sexual revolution. It wasn't a perfect world either. Sure, people didn't have the access to all the junk we have now, but that doesn't mean that everyone back then was living out God's view of sex either.

People had sex outside of marriage then. People looked at porn then. People lusted then. The youth of the first sexual revolution saw all of this and called society out on it. They saw people living one way secretly and another way publicly. And that just wasn't going to cut it.

Now everything's more visible. More open. More talked about. But we're still missing it.

So it's time for you to do something previous generations haven't done. It's time for you to get to the heart of what sex is really all about—not just anatomy, not just sensation.

You're not going to be able to follow a lot of people's leads on this. Your parents may have totally blown it. You may have a dad who has his own private movie collection. You may have a mom who doesn't think it's a big deal to flirt a little bit. You may know firsthand that the first sexual revolution didn't work because you have to deal with it every day within the four walls of your house.

You can't just follow every adult's lead, because many adults have done a really poor job at living this out. Since the world previous generations have created for you isn't exactly that great, whose lead are you going to follow?

Believe it or not: Jesus.

sex180

Of all the revolutions in history, one was started thousands of years ago—and it's still going.

Just like the revolutions that preceded it, it was started by someone who saw something that was wrong in the world, someone who knew there was a better way to do things than what was being done. He set out to change the world.

But this revolution didn't involve a war. It didn't involve one group of people taking power over another. In fact, this revolution was so unique that it hasn't been duplicated since. It was a revolution of the heart. The leader? Jesus Christ, the first true revolutionary.

Jesus saw what was broken around him. He saw humanity trying to deal with its biggest issue—sin—and failing time and time again. He saw a group of people who desperately needed to move beyond just knowing about God to having a personal relationship with him.

Of all the revolutions in history, one was started thousands of years ago—and it's still going.

There was only one way to do that. There was only one way to show God's love in a way that had never been shown before. It meant Jesus laying his life on the line. It meant paying a price that was too high for any one man or woman to pay.

Jesus knew that all the external ways of dealing with sin, ways which the Old Testament called the law, did nothing more than show people how sinful they really were. They needed a better way to live, but it couldn't happen without some divine intervention. Humanity needed some major catalyst to help us live our faith from the inside out rather than from the outside in. We needed more than external rules—we needed to see God's heart in a whole new way.

Jesus called out people who seemed to have it all together in public but lived a completely different way privately:

who, me?

> Woe to you, teachers of the law and Pharisees, you hypocrites! You are like whitewashed tombs, which look beautiful on the outside but on the inside are full of dead men's bones and everything unclean. In the same way, on the outside you appear to people as righteous but on the inside you are full of hypocrisy and wickedness.
>
> Matthew 23:27–28

Jesus also challenged people to treat one another with a level of love and respect beyond the ways they were treating each other. He asked them to love one another in revolutionary ways:

> I tell you: Love your enemies and pray for those who persecute you, that you may be sons of your Father in heaven. He causes his sun to rise on the evil and the good, and sends rain on the righteous and the unrighteous. If you love those who love you, what reward will you get? Are not even the tax collectors doing that? And if you greet only your brothers, what are you doing more than others? Do not even pagans do that?
>
> Matthew 5:44–47

Jesus didn't just point out people's sin, bring it out into the open, and make it socially acceptable to continue doing whatever they were doing. He told them to do a 180.

When a woman who was caught in the act of adultery was brought before Jesus, most people expected him to start hurling stones—the punishment for that act. But he didn't. He showed mercy to her and said to the crowd, "If any one of you is without sin, let him be the first to throw a stone at her" (John 8:7). When the people started getting honest with themselves, they realized they couldn't throw the first pitch. In fact, they dropped their rocks and walked away.

So did Jesus tell the woman, "Don't worry about it. It's not a big deal. Just next time be more careful. It's not like you

sex180

murdered anybody"? No. In fact, in the midst of this moment filled with mercy, Jesus told her about a better way:

> Jesus straightened up and asked her, "Woman, where are they? Has no one condemned you?"
> "No one, sir," she said.
> "Then neither do I condemn you," Jesus declared. "Go now and leave your life of sin."
>
> John 8:10–11

Did Jesus love her any less because he asked her to quit settling for less than God's best? No. In fact, he loved her enough to speak the truth. He loved her enough to not only show mercy but also to challenge her to quit buying into the lies that had enslaved and destroyed her.

[the unexpected]

People didn't recognize Jesus as revolutionary. The expectations they had for him were political, social, religious, and physical. They wanted deliverance from Roman rule. They wanted a new political system, an earthly kingdom, established. They wanted rules enforced. They wanted to be healed of sickness and diseases. They wanted a different way of life.

And what they got was nothing like what they expected. Because of that, some of them built walls of anger so high that they couldn't see Jesus anymore.

But what awaited those who were able to see themselves and their world through Jesus's eyes was a life unlike any they had ever experienced before. They found what their souls were so desperately searching for. They found truth in the words of Jesus: "I have come that they may have life, and have it to the full" (John 10:10).

who, me?

Jesus is still remembered in history. Christianity is a worldwide movement. Those are facts. Jesus was revolutionary because he did something no one else had done or could do—he changed hearts.

And that's where the next revolution, the second sexual revolution, will begin as well.

Not in following a bunch of rules.

Not in a government-funded program.

Not in a religious pep rally.

This revolution begins in the heart—your heart.

Jesus was revolutionary because he did something no one else had done or could do—he changed hearts.

sex180

the revolution: one

heart of the revolution

5

Before you can even begin to think about changing the world, you first have to let God change you. And the only way to do that is to know his heart—what he says about sex and why.

No one is going to listen to a thing you have to say about sex unless you believe it yourself.

You have to do more than just regurgitate the messages you hear. It's not about just wearing a ring or a T-shirt. It's not about just saying "wait" and "no."

You have to own it. You have to believe it deep down. And the only way you're going to do it is to understand why God says what he says about sex and sexuality. You've got to come face-to-face with God's heart.

We want to arrange that meeting.

Mine (Chip's) happened when I was in college in a small town in West Virginia. I was a brand-new Christian. I prayed to receive Christ just before I went away to college. I understood that I had sinned, I had violated a holy God. I asked him to forgive me

Before you can even begin to think about changing the world, you first have to let God change you.

and come into my life. He started to transform my life, putting new desires in me. I actually wanted to get up and read the Bible and talk to him. But it was wreaking havoc with my social life.

I was playing basketball on a scholarship at a school that had four girls for every guy—and I was trying to live out this new life. I was feeling like, "God, I really want to obey you, but I'm dying inside. I'm up and down and in and out a failure. I don't know how long I can handle this."

I wanted to follow God. I wanted to be loved. I wanted to have a lasting relationship. But I wanted to have sex, and I wanted it now. Inside there was a war raging between God's way and my way.

Then God gave me a vision—not a mystical, dreamlike vision, but a glimpse of his heart. One night a young couple from the church I attended invited me over to their house for dinner after church. When you're a college student, you'll take a meal anywhere you can get it.

Dave and Lanny were in their late 20s and had two kids, a 4-year-old and a 2-year-old. After a 25-minute drive through the hills in my Volkswagen Bug, I arrived at their house—a small white house that was in need of a fresh coat of paint. I didn't think of Dave and Lanny as poor, but looking back I realize that they didn't have doors on some of the hallways, just sheets tied up to separate the rooms.

We sat around their old 1950s-style table and had a great home-cooked meal. During the meal, I caught Dave looking at Lanny, and I caught her looking back with a knowing smile. I knew they had a great relationship, but something more was going on.

I could feel the energy and the warmth in the room, as well as the sense of completeness and, well, wholesomeness. Even the little kids' eyes were lit up. And as we ate, something was happening inside of me.

the revolution: one

After the meal, they pushed the plates to the center of the table and asked, "Would you excuse us? We're learning a new family tradition." Then Dave and Lanny pulled back the sheets to the kids' bedroom, knelt at the side of the bed, and folded the little kids' hands. Dave talked for a few minutes about how Jesus loved them. It was very simple. Then all four of them prayed together.

Dave prayed first, followed by Lanny.

When the little kids prayed, my heart melted. Then the kids held their mom and dad so tight and said, "I love you, I love you, I love you."

Dave and Lanny then came out from behind the sheet. We had coffee and apple pie a la mode. We sat around the table and talked. And as I was sitting in that room, I saw what I had been searching for. I knew that this was what I wanted someday. I wanted a life filled with that kind of love.

When I got in my car and drove home, I had plenty of time to talk to God. I said, "God, this is what I really want—this kind of connection, this kind of love. Why can't I have that? Why are you torturing me? Why are you putting all these restrictions on me? I just don't get it!"

I didn't hear an audible voice, but the Spirit of God said as clearly as I've ever heard, "Chip, that's why I put all the restrictions on sex. You see, you can only get what they have when it's one man and one woman for all time. The energy that you saw flows out of a heart, spirit, emotional, and social connection that's rooted in me."

God continued, "Chip, it's not that I'm keeping something good from you. All these prohibitions about immorality, about what you think, about lust—it's all about giving you my very best. I'm not trying to withhold pleasure; I created it. I created you. I want you to have what they have. Every command in Scripture is my attempt to protect you so that you'll get it."

heart of the revolution

My prayer wasn't just, "I know I've got to obey you, and I want to obey you, but you're asking me to do some stuff I don't like." It moved beyond just, "If I do this, you're going to discipline me." All the answers started fading away, and I saw something much deeper.

I realized that God was on my side. He wasn't fighting me. He wasn't holding out on me. The fences and the boundaries in my life were his loving arms holding me. He was trying to help me get the very best.

Romans 8:32 came to my mind: "He who did not spare his own Son, but gave him up for us all—how will he not also, along with him, graciously give us all things?" I felt like God was saying, "Chip, wake up! If I love you enough to give you my Son Jesus to die for you, do you think I'm going to withhold a great relationship? Do you think I'm going to withhold great sex? Do you think I'm going to withhold a lasting relationship? Chip, do it my way."

A light came on. I did a 180 on how I saw the whole thing. From that moment on, things were different. It doesn't mean I didn't struggle. It doesn't mean I never had a lustful thought. It doesn't mean I didn't make some mistakes, but from that moment on, I knew I wanted to do life God's way.

I had seen his heart—not only about sex but for me. I saw that he desired to give me good things.

The Bible says, "Every good and perfect gift is from above, coming down from the Father of the heavenly lights" (James 1:17). Jesus said in Matthew 7:9–11 that God desires to give us good gifts.

Sex is a good gift. God desires us to have it. He desires for us to enjoy all that sex can be—to experience it to its fullest potential. But before we can do that, we have to move beyond all the standard Christian answers and all the lies of our culture. We need to do a complete 180, running straight into God's heart.

Otherwise, it's another set of rules. It's just someone else's "do" and "don't do" list. Everyone's got one. Everyone has some kind of standard they live by. But what takes it to the next level is when you realize that behind the rules is someone who honestly, genuinely gives a rip about you. You'll follow that person. You'll live by the rules. You'll trust him or her because you know that person is not trying to control you. He or she isn't on a power trip. This person really, honestly cares.

Sex is a good gift. God desires us to have it.

That's why we need to see God's heart.

This is key. The revolution, the sex180, has to begin with each one of us. Individually, we have to get this. It has to be a revolution of one before it can even begin to affect others. There has to be a revolution "in" us before one can happen through us.

We have to understand why God says what he says about sex. We need a revolutionary way to think about sexuality—and for that we need something major to get us heading in the opposite direction. We need a full-on collision with God's heart.

[sex180: sex is sacred]

God says sex is sacred. Try saying that in your next conversation around the lunch table. Or bring that up the next time someone asks you why you don't watch certain movies. It'll get a few reactions. Most people think sex is a lot more common and basic than that. But God thinks it's more special.

The sacredness of sex means that God thinks sex is holy. *Uh, right*, you might be thinking.

But check out Hebrews 13:4: "Marriage should be honored by all, and the marriage bed kept pure, for God will judge the adulterer and all the sexually immoral." God says marriage is

heart of the revolution

to be honored. It's not simply to be appreciated. It's special! It's sacred! It's set apart for a specific time with a special person to deliver a special and sacred bond.

Not just appreciated. Not just wished for. Honored. Treated with respect.

And how do you do that? By keeping the marriage bed—the act of sex between two married people—pure. This isn't a someday thing. This is a now thing. The ways you think about sex now affect your future. They affect your marriage bed and what kind of experiences and memories you bring into it.

Big stuff. That's why sex can never be treated as common or casual. It's serious business to God.

The way we use and think of sex ultimately comes down to seeing it either as one of God's gifts or as a way to satisfy our own selfish desires. Sex outside of God's ideal of marriage (the lusting, taking, "I've got to have it" using of people) takes God out of the picture completely. The Bible says, "There's more to sex than mere skin on skin. Sex is as much spiritual mystery as physical fact. As written in Scripture, 'The two become one.' . . . We must not pursue the kind of sex that avoids commitment and intimacy, leaving us more lonely than ever—the kind of sex that can never 'become one'" (1 Corinthians 6:16–17 Message).

Listen to what Paul wrote to the church in Rome. (Think Roman Empire. Orgies. Temple prostitutes. Stuff like that was going on in every city Paul wrote to, not just Rome.) "God gave them over in the sinful desires of their hearts to sexual impurity for the degrading of their bodies with one another. They exchanged the truth of God for a lie, and worshiped and served created things rather than the Creator" (Romans 1:24–25).

They were willing to settle for a cheap imitation of what God intended. They worshiped sex instead of the God who gave it. They completely cut God out of sexuality, saying, "This has nothing to do with you. We'll take it from here. You stay out of this part of our lives." They made that part of God's creation into an idol to be worshiped by misusing the gift. We've made the same mistake.

At the heart of sex outside God's boundaries is an attitude of worship—worshiping yourself. Ultimately that kind of sex is a worship of my needs, my rights, my lust, and me. It has nothing to do with love and everything to do with fulfilling your own personal desires in your own time and in your own way. Paul wrote to the Ephesians,

> Be imitators of God, therefore, as dearly loved children and live a life of love, just as Christ loved us and gave himself up for us as a fragrant offering and sacrifice to God. But among you there must not be even a hint of sexual immorality, or of any kind of impurity, or of greed, because these are improper for God's holy people. Nor should there be obscenity, foolish talk or coarse joking, which are out of place, but rather thanksgiving.
>
> Ephesians 5:1–4

Paul says this to the Christ-followers in Ephesus who are living in a sex-saturated world with all these prostitutes—male, female, heterosexual, and homosexual—and all this weird and warped stuff going on. He says you are now children of the light. Don't participate in it. Don't even talk about what goes on in those temples or your own past experiences. You've got enough curiosity in your mind, so don't even go there. Not even close—not even a hint. Why? Because sex is sacred.

At its most intimate, sex is about *knowing*, not lying or sleeping together. When Adam and Eve began to explore their sexuality, the Bible described their intercourse by saying, "Adam knew Eve" (Genesis 4:1 KJV). The moment was sacred, holy. Each one of them, in God's design, was revealing the most sacred parts of their lives to one another—spiritually, physically, emotionally.

Much later in the Bible, when King David sinned by committing adultery with Bathsheba, a different word was used for the same physical act: David "lay with her" (see 2 Samuel 11:1–5 NASB). Although David knew Bathsheba was another man's wife, he lusted after her as an object and took her as a plaything. The consequences were horrendous and left behind a string of destroyed lives.

Sex isn't just about body parts fitting together or a momentary rush—it's about heart and personhood. It's about mystery. It's about sacredness.

Sex was never meant to sell stuff. Sex was never meant to get a cheap laugh. Sex was never something to be viewed casually as if for entertainment. It's a special, sacred, holy thing.

Not much is sacred in our culture. We hold very little in such high esteem. The Bible even predicted our world would be like this: "In the last days there will be very difficult times. . . . They will consider nothing sacred" (2 Timothy 3:1–2 NLT). In our efforts to talk about sex and be more open about it, we've let sex become too common. We've grown numb to what a huge deal this is. We've talked about it, written about it, sung about it, and seen it so much that it's become mundane. Nothing's sacred about it. We only realize its worth when we wake up one day and realize we settled for something much less than the best.

> **What would your life look like if you really believed that sex is sacred?**

That's why God shouts that sex is sacred. That's why what God says about sex is revolutionary. That's why it's a 180 from our world, even our own mindsets. Before we go on, let this sink in.

What would your life look like if you really believed that sex is sacred?

How would it affect what you watch? How you talk? What you listen to?

How would it alter what you do when you're by yourself? How would it affect what you think about?

the revolution: one

What would it change about what you do when you and another person are alone together?

The sacredness of sex is meant to be lived out daily in our minds, in our hearts, and especially in our souls.

[sex180: sex is serious]

Not only is sex sacred, but God's heart about sex is that it's serious too.

Sex can't be treated lightly. It's an expression of our deepest human commitment. It should include mystery and holiness and awe.

I (Chip) remember developing a friendship with a fellow player (I'll call Jimmy) on an outreach basketball team a number of years ago. We traveled and played together throughout South America. Most of the players were great players from big-name schools. We competed against amateur and Olympic teams, sharing our faith during the extended halftimes of the games.

We ended up rooming together. We hit it off great. Along with his athletic skills, Jimmy was an easygoing, great-looking guy who seemed to be enjoying the experience. As I got to know him, I found out that in addition to using his b-ball skills, he also played minor league baseball during the summer.

When we started talking about our own spiritual journeys, Jimmy surprised me with how open and honest he was. He said, "You know, it's so good to be a part of this. Most summers I'm busy playing pro ball." Then he added thoughtfully, "Finally, God got my attention."

"What do you mean?" I asked.

He said, "Well, I guess the best way to describe it is that I've been an idolater. I've spent all my life so far worshiping me. I never saw it that way before, but a few months ago I realized it's

heart of the revolution

what I have been doing." I wasn't sure how to respond. After a few moments he realized a little more info was needed.

"When I began playing on the road," Jimmy continued, "I got a real buzz from the crowd and I discovered I was attractive to ladies." He shook his head as if remembering something painful. "You know, as we moved from town to town all over America, there were times I had sex multiple times a day with different women. They were there, ready and waiting, after the games. And then at school, as a big basketball star, sex was a perk. At first, it was the game outside the game—how often and with how many different co-eds could I have sex? I lost count of the number. My life revolved around sex." There wasn't a hint of bragging in his voice. The words came from him slowly and shamefully, like terrible weights he wanted to drop.

"I went through about three years of this. Then I woke up one day and I was numb." Jimmy stopped for a moment, allowing me to absorb the significance of his confession. "I didn't feel anything. I didn't know who I was anymore. I didn't know how to have a relationship. I was like someone who stuck his hand in a fire over and over. The first few times, the jolts were memorable. But once the hand got burned enough and the nerves died under the ugly scars, the hand stopped feeling. My body actually came to the point that it didn't respond. I was a sexual burnout. My heart got dull, my brain couldn't respond." I will never forget his tone of deep sadness and his voice as he murmured, "There's a tiny piece torn from me that I left with each of those women that I can never get back." He described his years of indulgence in selfish sex by comparing it to being a piece of cardboard. Every time he had sex he was being glued to another piece of cardboard just long enough for the glue to dry. When the pieces were pulled apart, neither piece of cardboard came away whole.

"There are pieces of me all over with these women everywhere," Jimmy said. "I don't even know who I am, and I don't know how to have a relationship." Then he concluded with a flood of tears, "I got to where I didn't enjoy sex and I didn't like me. I was so far from God that I knew I was lost. Getting invited on this trip was God's gracious answer to my cry for help. As we go from country to country, I'm also on a spiritual journey. I'm asking God little by little to heal me."

Some of you may read this and envy Jimmy's skills and superstar status, the "rock star" position of nameless and faceless sex, and the ability to satisfy every urge as it came long.

But sex isn't casual. It's not common. Sex is sacred, and sex is serious. Both are key components in how and why God created sex in the first place. That's the deal.

The church in Corinth had big problems with sex and sexuality. If someone called you a "Corinthian girl," they were calling you a prostitute. This affluent town was one big party 24/7, with every kind of sexual pleasure available.

So when Paul wrote to the Christ-followers in the city of Corinth about the serious nature of sex, he was writing to people who were struggling to live out their faith in a world that just didn't see what the big deal was.

> Do you not know that your bodies are members of Christ himself? Shall I then take the members of Christ and unite them with a prostitute? Never! Do you not know that he who unites himself with a prostitute is one with her in body? For it is said, "The two will become one flesh." But he who unites himself with the Lord is one with him in spirit.
>
> Flee from sexual immorality. All other sins a man commits are outside his body, but he who sins sexually sins against his own body. Do you not know that your body is a temple of the Holy Spirit, who is in you, whom you have received from God? You are not your own; you were bought at a price. Therefore honor God with your body.
>
> 1 Corinthians 6:15–20

Sex isn't casual. It's not common. Sex is sacred, and sex is serious.

heart of the revolution

Paul's talking about sex with a prostitute here. People don't go to prostitutes for an emotional connection. They pay for sex because they simply want something physical. But Paul is saying, no matter how casually you view this, no matter how much you think you can cut out the emotional and spiritual part of this, you can't. The hookup arouses emotions, desires, and longings that are much too big and too powerful to be contained in a casual relationship—you need a lifelong commitment to handle them.

When two people have sex, whether they're married or not, even if it's a hookup, or whatever, the Bible says they not only merge body parts, they merge souls. That's how powerful and serious sex is.

That's why no matter how casual the relationship is, no matter how much two people are in agreement that they will not become emotionally involved, it will never work. Sex can never be just a physical thing. It's too serious and too sacred. It's too complex. It's not just another part of a relationship. It's not just some release. It's a connection that is binding.

When two people meet each other in sexual intercourse, a bond of the flesh occurs that goes beyond skin-to-skin. It's a life-uniting act. It's not a game; it's a life-altering decision. That's how serious sex is.

If you've already crossed the line—whether it's actual intercourse or some other sexual act with another person—you know what we're talking about here. What you did may have felt good at the moment, but something changed afterwards. Either for you or the other person or both—at some point, someone realized that there was a deeper connection made. That's why a piece of you died when he or she left. That's why what seemed like something that wasn't a big deal before became such a big deal later.

He or she (or you) didn't just walk away with a sexual memory; you both took pieces of each other's souls and now carry them around with you for life. That act, that memory, that person will be a part of your future marriage bed. You will bring that experience with you, no matter how great or awful it was.

God does offer forgiveness. He does offer hope and restoration. But the consequences of your sexual encounters, the realities of this life-uniting act, are something that you may carry with you forever. God loves you so much. He desires to protect you. Trust us—submitting to God's protection is better than falling apart and having to be put back together.

Sexual impurity destroys relationships. The first relationship it destroys is our relationship with God. People who progressively continue in sexual immorality are really saying, "I'm going to worship me." And that means they don't worship God. People are actually shocked to discover that fact. We shove God over to a little corner of our lives and instruct him to wait quietly until we get around to recognizing he's there and who he is. Worship is exclusive—you can only worship one "god," whatever your god is. We can't make life all about us and then expect God to fall in line. Our sin breaks our fellowship with God. It affects us deeply.

Remember the last time you knowingly stepped over one of God's boundaries? Perhaps nothing happened immediately. You may have even concluded you had a lot of fun. But how was your prayer life after that? Did you feel close to God?

James 4:8–10 says: "Draw close to God, and God will draw close to you. Wash your hands . . . purify your hearts. . . . Let there be tears for the wrong things you have done. Let there be sorrow and deep grief. . . . When you bow down before the Lord and admit your dependence on him, he will lift you up and give you honor" (NLT).

God knows the seriousness of sex and that if you disrespect its boundaries, sex will destroy your relationship with him. It won't separate you from his love (we'll talk more about that in the next chapter), but it will certainly cause a major gap in your relationship.

That's God's heart behind sex. That's why it affects how you think about sex now. Sex is sacred and serious when you're online, when you're at the movies, when you're listening to music, when you're watching TV. And since sex saturates so much of our culture, it's key that you live out your true sexuality—the way God created it—in every area of your life.

The sacredness and seriousness of sex is why "wait" and "no" just don't tell the full story. We need to know the *why*.

And when you know God's heart, when you realize that what he has to say is backed up by a true desire for your best interests, you'll find it easier to believe him and trust what he's saying is really true.

The sacredness and seriousness of sex is why "wait" and "no" just don't tell the full story.

God's saying, "These boundaries are all about my love for you. I've got a great plan. There's a wonderful person who will look at you with a knowing smile. You can have a normal life that's whole and real. You can have real excitement without all the baggage, shame, or guilt. I want to bless you. I want you to be together emotionally, spiritually, and physically. I want you to enjoy life like you've never imagined. That's always been my plan. It's why I put up guardrails. I gave a few commands. Why? Because I don't just want the best for you—I want the very best."

That's why God says to be careful where you let your mind wander, to take every thought captive (see 2 Corinthians 10:5). That's why God says don't allow in even a hint of lust. That's why God says sex is for marriage—and even after you're married, don't forget how sacred and serious sex is.

That's the hope. That's an answer that endures when the wait gets long. That's a response imprinted on your heart when your body is saying everything but "no."

You can control the hormones.

You can draw the lines.

You can take every thought captive.

Because when you don't, the price is way too high. It costs more than getting pregnant or an STD. It costs more than tearing up a pledge card or turning in a "wait" ring. It costs more than getting kicked out of the V club or losing some credibility with your Christian friends.

Sex is serious and sex is sacred. It was never meant to be played around with. When you do, the players get played and the hookups leave scars. But people just aren't getting that. It's not what they hear. It's not what they see.

Someone needs to show the world a better way. That's why doing a sex180 affects not only the way you think about sex but the way you live it out—in the ways you interact and attract.

You've seen the lies.

You've seen the truth.

You've seen what's broken and what needs fixing.

Now let the next revolution—the second sexual revolution—start with you.

[the revolution inside]

- As you live your life, what are some ways you can apply these truths—that sex is sacred and serious—to how you think every day?
- How would your life look different if you lived like you really believed sex is sacred? That sex is serious? What would need to change drastically? What would require some minor adjustments?
- How would you be different (or not) from your family? Friends? Youth group?
- What would be revolutionary about your life?

heart of the revolution

- Who do you think could help you the most as you start this personal revolution? Who could stand by you, support you, and hold you accountable? Who could remind you of what's true when temptation feels like more than you can bear?
- Who or what is your biggest obstacle to your personal revolution? What person, relationship, or activity has the most power to "kill" the revolution that God is bringing about in you?

extreme makeover: inside edition

6

God's serious about sex and he thinks it's sacred.

"Okay, got it. Can we move on?"

Not yet.

Before you start packing that info away with all the other good Christian answers you've learned all your life—somewhere between those generic Sunday school responses that are more regurgitated than heartfelt and the Bible stories that seem like just that, stories—we've got some advice for you. *This isn't going away that easily.*

This isn't just more information in your already overcrowded, overstimulated brain. This isn't a pledge card you can leave tucked behind your driver's license. This isn't a promise ring that you can leave in your jewelry box.

This isn't just an alternate way to live. You can't just add this to your "don't" list of being a Christian. You know what we mean—"I don't do drugs, drink, go to parties, cuss, or have sex because I'm a Christian."

This stuff will haunt you—because it's truth. Not because you've bought into a trend or even because you've bought this book. Not because it's guilt or manipulation.

You've seen God's heart. You can't walk away from that—not even one degree. Because if you do, you're denying not only the true nature of sexuality but also who you are. In order to have sex, you would have to make a decision to shut down some part of who you really are.

I (Tim) remember a time when I was away from home, away from family, and away from friends. In other words, I could do what I wanted and no one would even know what happened. What would happen there would stay there. I was in a strange city on a trip, working at a convention for my just-out-of-college job.

One particular day I had a random conversation with some-one who was working at a nearby booth. Something within me could tell that this person wasn't just making polite con-versation—they had an ulterior motive. I played dumb when an invitation was extended, but I knew that this person was looking for a hookup.

I was feeling lonely, so I played along. I had just been through a heartbreak—I was in love with someone, but she wasn't in love with me. I had attended more weddings in a three-month span than one heart could endure. I felt like everyone around me was finding the love of their lives, and I, like always, was left all alone. I didn't want to wait on God anymore. His timing wasn't so great, and I was getting tired of waiting.

I was desperate. I really wanted this quick fix to my loneli-ness. I wanted to be wanted. I wanted to be desired. I wanted to escape the fact that there was no "other" in my life. I wanted to find the love of my life, and since it wasn't happening, this seemed about as good as it would get. We met up later that night and I got what I wanted.

But every step of the way, with each new pick-up line, each new physical act, I knew that I was heading in the wrong direc-tion. I knew that what I was doing was setting aside everything I believed. I knew that God didn't approve, but I also knew that I wanted to be wanted.

And at one point, right before things went all the way, I started waking up. I started fighting my desires and started remembering who I really was. The inner struggle for my tainted purity came to a critical point and I said, "I can't do this." The hormones were going full blast. I had already gone much further than I ever should have. And it would have been really easy to just say, "I've already messed up. I may as well go ahead and just ask for forgiveness tomorrow," or to think that I owed it to this person to finish what we both had started.

But there was this haunting voice—the Holy Spirit reminding me of who I really am—that I just couldn't fully push away. I knew that if I kept going, some part of me would die there that night. And as much as I wanted to have all those needs and desires met that night, I knew hooking up was going to cost me so much more than I was going to gain.

I knew hooking up was going to cost me so much more than I was going to gain. So I left.

So I left. Even though the other person was really mad and tried to convince me that it wasn't that big of a deal, I knew in my heart it was. And I also knew that I had not only decided to take that path myself but had also led someone else down it with me.

That hookup had nothing to do with who I really was—God's child. He created me, even called me, to enjoy sex within the boundaries he created. Anything outside that was ignoring not only my identity, but all of the good things he had for me. As much as I thought I could disconnect my faith from my sexuality, it wasn't happening. It couldn't. It's inseparable.

I didn't want to be alone anymore, but God knew that my loneliness was a small price to pay in light of the sacredness and seriousness of sex. He knew that while nothing can separate me from his love, my sin—putting myself and my needs first, not God's—would pull me away from him. He knew that I would buy into the lie. And the guilt and shame would make me run further from him instead of to him.

If you get still enough and get honest enough with your own temptations or past experiences, you'll realize that too. It's what your heart's been telling you. Maybe you just can't hear it because our culture screams everything but that truth.

So now that you know the truth, now that you've seen what sex really is, what are you going to do with it? How is that going to affect how you live?

God knows that left on our own, we would settle for so much less. He knows that most of us would try to numb ourselves to the truth by walking around in denial with a huge gaping hole where our faith and our lives just don't connect. Not because we don't want to live differently but because we're scared, lazy, or just deceived. We don't want to step up and live in a way that's revolutionary.

But you can't walk away from truth. God holds you to it. The Bible says, "Anyone who listens to the word but does not do what it says is like a man who looks at his face in a mirror and, after looking at himself, goes away and immediately forgets what he looks like. But the man who looks intently into the perfect law that gives freedom, and continues to do this, not forgetting what he has heard, but doing it—he will be blessed in what he does" (James 1:23–25).

Jesus said it like this: "The thief comes only to steal and kill and destroy; I have come that they may have life, and have it to the full" (John 10:10).

So are you ready to live this out? Are you ready to let the revolution continue? Then it's time to let God's truth invade your life and start transforming not only the way you think (which is a daily process—see Romans 12:2) but also the way you live. It's time to connect the dots between your faith and your sexuality. It's time to let this truth revolutionize not only who you are but also how others see you.

So let the revolution continue—in you.

Now that you've had a glimpse into God's heart for sex and sexuality, it's time to take a look at another heart—yours. It's a place God's well acquainted with.

> O LORD, you have searched me
>   and you know me.
> You know when I sit and when I rise;
>   you perceive my thoughts from afar.
> You discern my going out and my lying down;
>   you are familiar with all my ways.
> Before a word is on my tongue
>   you know it completely, O LORD. . . .
>
> You created my inmost being;
>   you knit me together in my mother's womb.
> I praise you because I am fearfully and wonderfully made;
>   your works are wonderful,
>   I know that full well.
> My frame was not hidden from you
>   when I was made in the secret place.
> When I was woven together in the depths of the earth,
>   your eyes saw my unformed body.
>
> Psalm 139:1–4, 13–16

You know who wrote that psalm? David. Yes, David. The guy who had a hookup with another guy's wife, got her pregnant, and then had her husband killed in battle so his death appeared like another wartime tragedy and would cover up David's sin.

He's also the same man the Bible describes as a man after God's own heart (see 1 Samuel 13:14). Even after he sinned sexually. It's not our past history that defines us but our future direction.

God knew David. He knew every weakness. He knew every desire—both good and bad—that lived in David's heart. David blew it big time, but a revolution started in David's heart after he saw his sin for what it was and cried out to God for forgiveness and a second chance (read Psalm 51).

And God knows you too. He's into the details of your life. He even knows how many hairs are on your head (see Matthew 10:30). He knows where you've been, what you've done, and what you've thought.

You can try to hide from him. You can pretend like God doesn't understand. But what's the point? He knows.

And yet here's the part that just blows our minds. Here's the part that just doesn't make sense. Sometimes the "too much information" of people's lives really makes it hard to love them. We see sides of people that make us want to walk away. But God sees past all our outside attempts at perfection. He sees the real us—and still desires a relationship with us. He even loves us! The apostle Paul wrote,

It's not our past history that defines us but our future direction.

> For I am convinced that neither death nor life, neither angels nor demons, neither the present nor the future, nor any powers, neither height nor depth, nor anything else in all creation, will be able to separate us from the love of God that is in Christ Jesus our Lord.
>
> Romans 8:38–39

This isn't a superficial love that says "whatever" to your worst traits. This is the kind of love that says, "I'm not going anywhere. I love you and I am staying right here. You've got some big issues, big problems, but I'm going to walk through them with you. Not because you have to change in order for me to love you, but because I love you too much to leave you stuck there." It's the kind of love that empowers you. It's the kind of love that frees you.

the revolution: one

You can discover all you were meant to be with that kind of love backing you up. You can trust that the boundaries have a purpose. You can trust that the correction is meant to get you back on track. You can trust that the wait is part of a much bigger plan. You can quit searching for the guy or girl of your dreams and become the person you were meant to be.

How does that happen?

You pursue God. Don't worry. He's going to let you catch him. He promises, "You will seek me and find me when you seek me with all your heart" (Jeremiah 29:13).

You walk with him. You choose daily to say, "I'm going to live your way, not mine. I want you to be a part of everything I do, think, and say today." Psalm 26:3 says, "Your love is ever before me, and I walk continually in your truth."

You trust him. When life seems like a total mess, you believe that he's doing something much bigger than just solving your crisis. "As the heavens are higher than the earth, so are my ways higher than your ways and my thoughts than your thoughts" (Isaiah 55:9).

You don't just listen to a sermon or read your Bible—you live it out. "Anyone, then, who knows the good he ought to do and doesn't do it, sins" (James 4:17).

Your first and foremost desire is for God to make you into who he wants you to be, not into who you think others want you to be. "Search me, O God, and know my heart; test me and know my anxious thoughts. See if there is any offensive way in me, and lead me in the way everlasting" (Psalm 139:23–24).

This doesn't mean you're going to be perfect. It doesn't mean you always make the right choices. But it does mean that you want what God wants more than what you want. You're willing to sacrifice your desires and your dreams, to be a living sacrifice (see Romans 12:1), because you realize that your brain and your skills are limited. There's only so far you can take yourself. There's only so much you can be on your own.

the internal world

Maybe you're thinking, "Guys, my problem is that sex is all actually about me. I've got the dealing with other people thing down fine. I've drawn lines that I have no intention of crossing. But inside my head is a different story. I'm not lusting after everybody I see. But when I'm solo, sometimes I think about my future wife. No one in particular, just that special someone and what I want to do with her. I like to fantasize about what sex with her will be like someday. That's okay, right?"

It actually depends on how detailed you're getting. You see, the more you think things up, the bigger your expectations are. So what you think is helping you buy some time while you're trying to do the right thing could be packing some extra baggage for your future honeymoon. Plus, the whole fantasy thing fuels that lust that's always lurking, waiting to get some kind of hold on your life.

The someday will be good. The adventure will be amazing. But in the meantime, remember what Paul told the Corinthians—it's like a war cry—"We take captive every thought to make it obedient to Christ" (2 Corinthians 10:5).

What goes on in your head is just as key as what happens on the outside. Read Matthew 5:28–29.

Remember, Jesus said he came not only to give you life but to give it to the full (see John 10:10). The Bible also says, "No eye has seen, no ear has heard, no mind has conceived what God has prepared for those who love him" (1 Corinthians 2:9).

When you entrust your life to God's hands, living out his commands, you become a man or woman of character. You become the kind of person he can entrust the care of another person to.

the revolution: one

While God is trading spaces on the inside of your life, he also wants to do a makeover on the outside. He wants the things he's doing in your heart, your life, and your character to be reflected in how you appear to others.

How you look is what catches the attention of those around you. And let's be honest here—it feels really good to be noticed. We want to be desired and wanted. We're attracted to other people, and we want others to find us attractive.

You can look in the mirror in the morning and think, *I look good today,* but when someone else tells you how good you look, you soar. That's why a lot of people go to some extreme measures to make sure they capture the attention of those around them. With so many people trying to get noticed, the competition for a second glance is fierce. That's why skin is in and tight is supposedly right.

In describing her outfit, which included a tight, black tube top, Karen from Virginia admits, "Clothing like this makes me feel confident. People's eyes are on me, not on the other girl."[1]

That's the current way to attract. It's all about sex appeal, physical attraction, dressing seductively, and focusing on your body. It's the way people dress at school and even at church.

But it's what I like to wear, you may be thinking. *It's just the style.* Simge, wearing snug lime-green pants and a white halter top, says that when she looks in the mirror, she thinks, *You look good. I'm comfortable with myself. I don't ask anyone else.*[2]

It's a personal choice, right? If people have a problem with it, they just need to get over it, right?

Makes sense, but you forgot something—the world's not all about you. What you wear affects

Sex appeal, physical attraction, dressing seductively, and focusing on your body. It's the way people dress at school and even at church.

others—and honestly, you know that. You know how good it feels to be noticed.

In the area of modesty, we've bought the lie. We may never say it verbally, but we sure do advertise messages like, "Hey, look at my boobs, not my face!" "Have you seen my butt?" "I've got a six-pack," or "Check out my pecs."

And when you throw that kind of bait out there, you're going to get what you're advertising for. You're going to get the kind of guy or girl who's more concerned with how you look than who you are. Sure, that feels good. But these aren't people who see the real you. These aren't people who desire to know you. These are people who desire to use you.

Do you want a good guy or girl? Do you want someone of character and substance? Do you want someone who is pursuing this revolution just as much as you?

God's 180 way to attract that kind of person is this: "Your beauty should not come from outward adornment, such as braided hair and the wearing of gold jewelry and fine clothes. Instead, it should be that of your inner self, the unfading beauty of a gentle and quiet spirit, which is of great worth in God's sight" (1 Peter 3:3–4).

The Bible's not advocating a new style here. The verse is saying that if you want to be attractive, if you want to be the kind of guy or girl who turns heads, attract with something of substance. Attract with something that you can't get at the mall. Work out the inside of your heart just as much as you work out the outside of your body. Show your character, not your boobs or butt.

We're all trying so hard to appear perfect on the outside. To be the "after" on some makeover show. To be the kind of person others would drool over in a fashion magazine. We're afraid to just be ourselves. We're afraid to let everyone see who we really are, so we try to divert their attention to somewhere else.

the revolution: one

Eric posted the following message on the YouthWalk website:

> "Pop culture makes you think that to have a good relationship with your bf/gf, you need to be perfect on the outside. They make you think that if that happens, your social life will be perfect too. But the truth is, sometimes it's better not to be so perfect because when you have outer flaws your friends love you for who you are. And especially with a bf/gf, you have a more real connection because then it's about more than the other person's body."

Eric is right. It's about being a person who is real. About being a person who attracts others based on what God thinks about sex and sexuality—that it's sacred and serious.

Imagine what would happen if you sat down with three or four close friends whose walk with God you deeply respect and discussed what you wear and why. What if you actually talked about how low cut is too low, how short or tight you should wear your clothes, and why? What if a few guys openly questioned one another's motives for pumping iron or driving around wearing muscle shirts (or no shirts) and kept each other accountable for healthy living?

When a girl puts a sweater on and murmurs, "I wonder how that looks through the eyes of a guy?" or when a guy sticks on a tight shirt after he's been pumping iron and asks himself, "Will the girls notice what I've been doing?" these are signs of our addiction to our culture.

God gave us wonderful and beautiful bodies. They were not intended for manipulating others. The changes in your physical body that have occurred (and are still occurring) may change the way people notice you and even the way you see others—but those changes don't alter the way God sees you. Don't reduce all of who you are to just what people see. Make the connection between your closet and your faith so that people can see your beliefs in action, not your navel. *That* will attract people's attention.

When Tim's friend Laurin got the following email from a guy after a church beach retreat, she wasn't quite sure what to think after reading the first line: "I have a bone to pick with you." But when Laurin kept reading, she knew that God was sending some divine encouragement her way:

> I think there are a lot of people, particularly guys, who are missing you and what you're about. I want you to know that I'm not. I notice how you live your life. At the church beach retreat, I noticed that you were the only girl in a one-piece—and you certainly don't have a need to cover anything up. But I really appreciated what you wore. I'm saying all of this because I want you to know that I really like the way you honor God with the way you live your life. You love him, and I can tell. As your brother in Christ, I find it extremely encouraging, incredible, and attractive.

For some of you the revolution would start by looking through your closet for what not to wear. It would start by throwing out those shirts that you buy one size smaller. It would start by trashing those outfits that force you to suck in your gut the whole time you're wearing them.

The next sexual revolution requires a group of people who will get rid of all that junk and say, "I'm going to dress attractively—very sharp and stylish—but not seductively because there's more to me than that."

Make the connection between your closet and your faith so that people can see your beliefs in action, not your navel. *That* will attract people's attention.

[upward devotion]

Besides your sense of style, do you know something else that makes you attractive? Your upward devotion to God.

the revolution: one

Something is very appealing about a guy or girl who is genuinely in love with Jesus. Someone who is passionately pursuing God. Someone who realizes that the missing gaps in his or her life are filled with God first—he's where they find completion.

I (Chip) remember the first time I asked my wife, Theresa, out on a date. She said that she couldn't go because she had a previous commitment. I wondered how she could have any previous commitment more important than the chance to spend time with me. (I suffered from a warped view of my own importance.)

Being the curious guy I was, I drove by her house that night, wondering if I had some potential competition from another guy. Her car was the only one in the driveway, and the lights were on in the living room—she was obviously at home. I reacted with some anger followed quickly by a pang of rejection. I thought she was an amazing woman who was actually interested in me. So how could she choose to spend an evening alone at home rather than being with me?

Two days later my wrong assumptions were corrected by one of her friends. She told me Theresa had shared with her how difficult it had been to turn me down. She had set the evening aside to spend time alone with God.

As a result of a very difficult time in her life, Theresa had developed the habit of spending several hours during a couple of evenings per week in prayer and personal communication with God—reading the Bible, singing, and enjoying his presence.

The rejection I had felt turned instantly to attraction. How could I not want to be with someone who was committed to her relationship with God in the same way I longed to be?

When I realized I was turned down because God was more important in her life, something clicked inside that I couldn't explain. Somehow, being second to God was both a relief and a great attraction.

When the object of your affection is going to God first for what he or she needs, it takes the pressure off. You don't have to be his or her everything. And the truth is, you were never meant to be. You'll never measure up.

"Everybody thinks that if you're in a relationship everything's fine," Audrey declares. "That's totally not the way it is. I'm really blessed to have the boyfriend I have at this time in my life, but that's not what fulfills me at all. When I'm alone and totally focused on God—that's what matters. That's what makes me happy. That's what brings me joy.

"I've been going through a tough time lately, and my boyfriend's been trying to help. He asked me, 'Why are you still so unhappy?'

"I told him, 'Because it doesn't come from you. I have to get this from God.' It's something I wish everybody realized; then maybe they wouldn't spend all their efforts on trying to find a boyfriend, because they are just going to look and look to try to find someone who won't be that."

A bf/gf will never be your Savior. There's only one Savior, Jesus Christ.

If you want to build a lasting relationship, you'll need more than great hair, a buff body, and a good tan. Those things fade quickly and are rather superficial. But when you meet a person with upward devotion, you realize they have substance, character, and a beauty that won't perish with time. It's the kind of person you want to seek out, and it's the kind of person you want to be.

A bf/gf will never be your Savior. He or she won't save you from your loneliness, your family, your stress, your insecurities. None of that will ever be satisfied by another person. There's only one Savior, Jesus Christ. He desires your undivided devotion.

As you think about becoming the person God wants you to be and attracting the opposite sex as part of this second sexual revolution, remember IOU:

Inward character
Outward modesty
Upward devotion

This IOU will involve some major God-honoring tactics. You may need to throw away some clothes, evaluate your outward appearance, and analyze some of your habits. But remember this: the outside should be a clear reflection of the inside—a deep desire to please God. This isn't a style issue as much as it's a heart issue.

Regardless of your taste in clothes, the core issue for this sex180 needs to be *What am I seeking to communicate by how I dress or how I look?* Ultimately, you need to be able to explain how your external actions and even style are an expression of your upward devotion to God.

When you and I look in the mirror, we need to prayerfully consider Colossians 3:17: "And whatever you do, whether in word or deed, do it all in the name of the Lord Jesus, giving thanks to God the Father through him." Every part of our lives can express our debt of gratitude to God as we seek to develop an inward character, outward modesty, and upward devotion that represent that we belong to the one who gave his life for us.

We don't owe our culture, our peers, or even ourselves anything like the debt of gratitude we owe to the Lord Jesus Christ. You may need help in figuring out the specifics of what that looks like in your life. It's not about what others think or about being conservative or even about pleasing important adults in your life—it's about daring to live a revolutionary life because we desire to please God and do relationships his way.

Are we saying that looking good, pumping iron, and taking care of our bodies is wrong? Absolutely not! We don't have a problem with people looking good or even good-looking people. The problems come when we rely on how we look as our primary tool for attracting and impressing others.

When we make it our lifestyle to develop inward character, outward modesty, and upward devotion, we actually allow our bodies to fulfill their best purposes. Our IOU continues to flourish and become even more beautiful as the years roll by, long after the physical shell has suffered the effects of time. When we base relationships on what is passing and fading, we make those relationships vulnerable to time. But God offers us revolutionary ways of thinking about lasting attraction between people—the truth.

[the revolution inside]

- What do you do to feel good about yourself (like go shopping, work out, etc.)?
- What makes you feel attractive?
- What do people notice about you?
- What do you wish people noticed about you?
- Based on what you've read in this chapter, in what ways do you need to alter your life to make sure people see you for the person God says you are—not what the mirror or our culture says?
- What person in your world could you honestly talk to about these revolutionary ways of living?
- Take some time today to talk to your mom or dad (or both) about the revolution that's going on inside you and how you're going to live out this 180.

the revolution: one

the revolution:
   one + one

relationships180

You've done a 180 on your own perception of your sexuality—what God says about it and how you live it out. But what happens when you add another person into the mix? What does it look like to live out a sex180 in your relationships? How can you enjoy time with the opposite sex and still stay true to what God says about who you are? How can you interact with others in a way that demonstrates your inward character, outward modesty, and upward devotion? How can you make sure your actions line up with your belief that sex is sacred and serious?

The answer: you live out the revolution. It's no longer just a revolution of one. It's a one + one revolution.

We have basically two ways to do relationships—God's way and Hollywood's way. Actually, it's more than just Hollywood. It also includes music, magazines, and books. But we'll just focus on Hollywood because it's a little hard to ignore the images on the big screen. (Plus, the formula is a big part of the plotlines to most romantic movies.)

According to Hollywood, four basic steps lead to deep, intimate, sizzling relationships. Before you start thinking we're going a little overboard, think about how these steps play into the plot of your favorite love story or the tabloid headline lives of your favorite stars. Then, if you really want to get honest, look at how these steps play out in your own expectations of love.

[hollywood step #1: find the right person]

The key to love is finding that one special person who was made just for you. He or she is out there. You just have to find him or her. Drive around. Hang out. Be on the lookout when you're at the mall, riding the bus, waiting at Starbucks, or saving the world. Dress, look, and act in a way that will demand his or her attention. The moment will come. You just have to keep looking.

[hollywood step #2: fall in love]

When you find the right person, something will click and you'll just know. Maybe it's something about the way he or she walks or talks. Maybe it's a brief look or gesture. Maybe he or she is so "hot" you just feel this undeniable attraction. You may not even know his or her name, but you'll know that you're in love.

Love is completely based on chemistry—not knowledge or character. You'll know you're in love because you'll have these mushy feelings and electrical pulses will surge all over your body. Unfortunately, your IQ will immediately drop about 30 points. You'll spend money you don't have. You'll spend time doing things that are ridiculous. This amazing, much-sought-after experience of "falling in love" means overwhelming feelings that throw out reason, background, shared interests, and even compatibility. After all, opposites attract, right? Love, says Hollywood, makes you crazy.

the revolution: one + one

Love is all that matters. You know it because emotions this strong, this sudden, and this overwhelming must be the real thing. The only choice seems to be to move on to the next step.

[hollywood step #3: fix your hopes and dreams on this person for your future fulfillment]

In the movies, love overrides every other decision. A virgin is willing to give him- or herself to another person because he or she has finally found true love. Brides and grooms are regularly left at the altar because their future mates have decided to run off with someone else with whom they are "really in love."

Once you fall in love, in the Hollywood version, every other promise you have made is null and void. You can't be held to any previous commitment. The person with whom you "fall in love" will become the object of your life, your future, your dreams, and your satisfaction. You have suddenly realized that this person and this person alone will make you complete. He or she will make you whole. Life will have meaning like it never has before (except for all the other times you've been in love).

You begin to believe you can't make it without him or her. You constantly daydream about this person, writing perfect, romantic scripts about your life together in your head. You fully expect that this person will be able to meet your deepest longings and needs and will come through for you 100% of the time. Though we know on some level that it's impossible, we've been taught that finding the right person will solve all our problems.

Hollywood also provides a convenient "Plan B" for when "true love" gets shaky. We "drift apart" or "fall out of love." It's "just not the same anymore." We're led to believe that falling out of love is just as natural and unexpected as falling in love. We either chose the wrong person, or we were right for each other for a season but that season has now passed. It has nothing to do with us.

And when that happens, it's time for step 4.

[hollywood step #4: if failure occurs, repeat steps 1, 2, and 3]

In the Hollywood version, step 3 (fixing your hopes and dreams on someone for your future fulfillment) usually leads to failure. Big surprise. Can you image how smothering it would be under the pressure to be someone's absolute everything? Whoa.

So when the relationship starts to break down, Hollywood offers an easy solution: go back to the beginning and start over. Repeat steps 1, 2, and 3. It's time once again to (1) find the right person, (2) fall in love, and (3) fix your hopes and dreams on this new and improved person you have found. This time maybe it will work. Just go on to the next partner, repeating steps 1–3. Think of it as the sequel to the first film. Same lead, different love interest.

Here's the premise behind it all: the key to love is finding the right person. If your current relationship isn't working out so great for you, if for some reason this person doesn't fulfill all your dreams and desires, then you must have the wrong person.

Basically, a normal relationship in our culture follows a very predictable pattern.

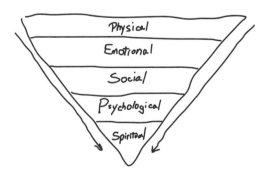

the revolution: one + one

1. Physical: It all begins with the physical. It's all about chemistry and attraction (and not the kind of attraction we mentioned in the IOU section). This is the starting point.

2. Emotional: The next phase is the great feelings, "falling in love" phase. It also tends to be filled with mood swings. Wild adoration can be followed almost instantly by insane jealousy. Because you just don't know a lot about the other person, you interpret anything he or she does solely by your own experiences—how people in your own past have reacted in the past—not necessarily based on the present reality.

3. Social: This is when you meet the family and/or friends. At this point you get either approval or dire warnings from the people in your life. But usually the couple moves on regardless of what anyone thinks or says. Nothing can be more "right" than what they feel, can it?

4. Psychological: At this point, the other three phases catch up and certain questions and needs arise in the relationship. This is usually the point where no matter how hard you've tried to make a good impression, the real you starts showing. The cracks in the relationship start showing too. The psychological stage is when most couples usually break up. When we start to see behind the makeup (or muscles), we often find a not-so-attractive person clothed in a very attractive body. And when that breakup happens, it's usually pretty brutal because the physical, emotional, and social connections have been made. Friends take sides. Emotions are out of whack. And memories of past physical contact with this person just leave you feeling used. The reality that the relationship has been built on a pretty shallow base is painfully evident (see chart).

5. Spiritual: Since God and personal faith haven't really been a part of the relationship till now, this is the point where the spiritual receives its invitation—at the wedding. God

is invited, but he's usually asked to be there in a very minor capacity—a small, walk-on, cameo role in the big production.

That's how most people do relationships—and it's so messed up, isn't it?

People are walking around looking like crash survivors, dazed and confused, in shock because of what just happened. "How did something so great turn so ugly?" they ask themselves. And it hurts. It hurts bad.

Is there a better way? There's got to be. We've got to be able to relate to the opposite sex in a way that isn't so brutal. We've got to find a way to do relationships that doesn't leave so many casualties.

We need something different. We need to find a way to interact that is both realistic and God-honoring. Not every person you're attracted to is going to be your future spouse. Not every relationship ends in marriage. And the alternative of hiding out and waiting for God to bring your Prince or Princess Charming to your doorstep isn't very realistic either. We need a new way to do relationships, a revolutionary way. We need a 180. Let's do a 180 on that Hollywood version. Let's flip it and work our way up from bottom to top in a whole different way. Reverse the numbers. Make Spiritual #1 and Physical #5 and you have a whole different ball game.

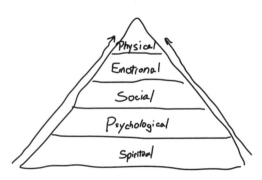

the revolution: one + one

The physical, emotional, social, psychological, and spiritual are all good components of a relationship. After all, they just mirror all the parts of who you are too. The problem with these phases is that they are usually completely out of order.

If you get the order right, you have a good foundation to get to know one another. The physical comes much later and doesn't complicate things. You let the other person see the real you up front, no games. Your emotions are held back until you know this person and his or her background a little better. The spiritual becomes the foundation of the relationship.

It certainly filters out the psychos.

The Bible talks about two commands that are at the core of loving people God's way:

> Be <u>imitators of God</u>, as beloved children; and <u>walk in love</u>, just as Christ also loved you and gave Himself up for us, an offering and a sacrifice to God as a fragrant aroma.
>
> Ephesians 5:1–2 NASB

Notice the underlines? Imitating God and walking in love are two core ways to live out God's 180 way to do relationships.

So how do you do that? Let's walk through what that looks like. As you're reading, make sure you link that IOU (inward character, outward modesty, upward devotion) to these steps. We think you'll see how crucial it is that you live those out before you're even ready to bring another person into the picture.

[God's 180 step #1: instead of looking for the right person, become the right person]

God tells us that instead of constantly looking for the right person, we should become the right person. Instead of looking for love, God tells us, we are to realize that love has already found us! Our love for others flows out of our sense of being deeply loved.

God loves us as no one else can. The best way for us to demonstrate that we get that is to learn to imitate him as closely as possible in the way we treat others. So what does that look like? Ephesians 4:32 tells us: "Be kind and compassionate to one another, forgiving each other, just as in Christ God forgave you."

Imitating God means that in relationships we are to be kind, tenderhearted, empathetic, discerning, willing to make allowance for people's mistakes, and consistently forgiving. It means we want good for others. We're gentle toward them even when our needs don't get met or when we're angry.

We let others off the hook because the truth is that they weren't meant to meet all of our needs. No one person can handle that task. We're a bottomless pit of needs and issues. Only God can be our Savior. So when someone lets us down or disappoints us, we do the unthinkable—we forgive them.

God's Word never discounts feelings, but it clearly defines love as having much more to do with character and action than feelings. In other words, genuine love causes us to do things that don't necessarily have good feelings attached to them. Jesus allowed himself to be nailed to a cross not because it felt good but because he loved us. We can spend a lifetime discovering the truth behind the simple thought in 1 John 4:19: "We love, because He first loved us" (NASB).

Our problem is that loving someone isn't easy. We simply don't have the power to always forgive or be consistently kind. Some of us are really grumpy sometimes. Our love, strength, will, and understanding can only be stretched so far. We don't have the power to love this way unless we are so filled with God's love that we recognize that our deepest needs have already been met through him and we're no longer expecting another person to "complete" us. We find that somewhere else.

See, we're not just "okay" to God. We're not just someone he puts up with or his second choice. In fact, through Jesus

Christ we are wonderful, significant, valuable, dearly loved, and the objects of God's infinite and unconditional love. The God who made us and loves us tells us to love like he loves us. This is why the idea of just finding the right person in order to have a great relationship is a lie.

In their book *Relationships*, Les and Leslie Parrott bring this point home clearly:

> If you attempt to build intimacy with a person before you've done the hard work of becoming a whole and healthy person, every relationship will be an attempt to complete the hole in your heart and the lack of what you don't have. That relationship will end in disaster.[1]

As a side benefit (but not the goal), by becoming more like Christ, you're going to attract someone with the same passion. Isn't that the kind of person you really want to find? Someone who will love you completely—both the good and the bad? Someone who is seeking to imitate God's love to everyone he or she encounters?

If it is, then become that kind of person first. That's something you can work on now—whether you're in a relationship or not.

[God's 180 step #2: instead of falling in love, walk in love]

Walking in love means something much deeper than taking long strolls on the beach or wandering hand-in-hand through the mall. In fact, walking in love means that we love others in exactly the same way that Christ loved us.

Walking in love means giving the other person what they *need* the most when it is least deserved, not necessarily giving what they *want* the most. That's exactly how God has treated you. That's what genuine love is.

When you walk in love, the relationship isn't all about you. It's not about your life or about what you can get. It's about how you can serve the other person. When you love this way, you're not easily angered. You don't blow up. You don't pout. Unlike Hollywood's version of love that depends on passionate feelings, good looks, and perfect circumstances, walking in love remains loyal and steadfast even in the worst of times. It's the kind of love that's not going anywhere, no matter what. Unfortunately, with over half of marriages ending in divorce, we don't see this in action too much.

Walking in love also means being honest with one another—sometimes painfully honest. It means caring enough to call someone out on something you see them doing, even if you know doing so may cause some pain and anger. It means sometimes saying or doing things that you know will make the other person mad—not for some sick pleasure but because you care too much to say "yes."

Don't fall in love. Walk in love.

Have you ever had a time when a friend, parent, or coach called you out on something? Your first reaction may have been to get mad or embarrassed. You probably thought, "What's your problem? Why is this such a big deal?" But deep down you knew they had seen something in you that they wouldn't let slip by because they cared too much. And they could have walked away and said, "That's your problem." But they didn't. They showed love to you by doing what was in your best interest, even if it was the last thing in the world you wanted to happen. And you probably knew that later. Once the emotions simmered down, you were glad they did or said what they did.

Love is a sacrificial, other-centered action that provides what's best for the other person. It means saying no to sex outside God's boundaries because that kind of physical connection has nothing to do with the two of you helping each other and everything to do with the two of you using each other.

the revolution: one + one

Don't fall in love, God tells us. Walk in love. Genuine love isn't a passive, quivering mass of good feelings. Genuine love is a deliberate, intentional, honest, and even painful giving up of self-preservation for another person's good.

[God's 180 step #3: instead of fixing your hopes and dreams on another person, fix your hope on God and seek to please him through this relationship]

In the Hollywood wedding ceremony, the couple stands face-to-face before their gathered friends. These ceremonies are often filmed on sets that look like places of worship even though God's not even given a small walk-on role in the ceremony. The couple basically declares, "You are the most important person in my life. You complete me. You are my perfect mate, the answer to all my dreams."

The 180 to that is a wedding where God takes the lead. He's the major star of the event, outshining even the bride. The couple acknowledges his place, and they expect him to help them keep the promises they make. But their view of one another could be expressed this way: "You are not the most important person in my life—Christ is. And because Christ is the most important person in my life, I'm going to treat you even better than I could treat you if you were the most important person in my life. Christ will help me love you more than I could ever love you in my own strength alone."

The goal of relationships isn't to make sure everything goes our way or makes us happy. The goal is to please God. The best our culture can offer as a model for marriage involves two people who are trying hard to please each other. God's 180 way is when two people are actually learning to please a third—God—by the way they respond to him and to each other.

When we go the other way and make our personal fulfill-ment the goal of every relationship, it never works out. And then we wrongly assume the problem is the other person, so we go and find someone else. Why do you think so many of those TV bachelors and bachelorettes just can't seem to find true, lasting love?

Instead of trying to find out what's wrong with the other person, instead of continually expecting him or her to conform to our needs, we must ask God to make us who he wants us to be and to help us to walk in love, giving sacrificially what the other person needs.

As long as we live with this warped idea that sets the other person up to meet all our expectations, we are doomed to disappointment. Great relationships involve struggle, conflict, working through issues, and refusing to demand—consciously or not—that the other person make our life work. The result is a lot of personal growth and a healthy relationship.

[God's 180 step #4: if failure occurs, repeat steps 1, 2, and 3]

The fourth step for God's 180 way is the same as Hollywood's—it just plays out differently. Both Hollywood and God's 180 recognize an inevitable feature of human relationships—failure. When it comes to failure in a relationship, the real question isn't if but when. When it happens, you go back to the beginning. You walk through the steps: imitate God, walk in love, fix your hope on God, and seek to please him in every one of your relationships.

Sounds good, you might be thinking, *but I'm not planning on getting married for a while—a long while. I'll keep that stuff in mind, but what am I supposed to do until then?*

That's your call. We're not saying relationships are bad. We're not telling you to kiss dating good-bye. We're not saying courting is the only solution. We're not even saying dating is that great either. What we are saying is that this is God's heart. And

the revolution: one + one

in the next chapter we'll flesh out what it might look like to live that out in your relationships.

This is revolutionary compared to everything you see or hear in our culture. It's revolutionary compared to the way most adults live out their relationships, and it certainly is revolutionary compared to the "ideals" we see in the media. It's revolutionary compared to the way most people approach relationships.

This revolution of one + one is all about keeping your heart in line with God's and helping someone else do the same. And to do that, you need to proceed in some revolutionary ways—well, at least revolutionary compared to the normal Hollywood stuff, because their methods aren't working out so great.

Just check out the tabloids. Listen to the entertainment shows.

Or just look at the students in your school. Or the relationships in your family.

The debris is everywhere. The carnage of hurting, painful relationships is carried by people so scared of reliving the pain, they will do anything to numb it—including making the same mistakes.

So how do you keep a relationship in line with God's heart every step of the way? When you really like someone but want to make sure you have a God-honoring relationship, what does that look like?

We're getting there. But before we move on, let the revolution continue in you.

This revolution of one + one is all about keeping your heart in line with God's and helping someone else do the same.

[the revolution inside]

- Which of the ways we talked about today represents the way you've done relationships in the past?

Hollywood's Way	God's 180 Way
1. Find the right person.	1. Become the right person.
2. Fall in love.	2. Walk in love.
3. Fix your hopes and dreams on this person for your future fulfillment.	3. Fix your hope on God and seek to please him through this relationship.
4. If failure occurs, repeat steps 1, 2, and 3.	4. If failure occurs, repeat steps 1, 2, and 3.

- What would you like your relationships to look like in the future?
- Looking at God's 180 way to do relationships, where have you made decisions in past relationships that took you off course? What could you do differently the next time around?

the revolution: one + one

real friends, real benefits

8

Hear that? It's the sound of people's souls rumbling—they're starving for relationships. It's how we're wired. Whether we want to admit it or not, we want to connect with another person in some kind of relationship—a friend, a date, a spouse. We want to meet someone who understands us and cares.

Why do you think we go to chick flicks (and yes, guys even tolerate a few of them)? We love the stories. We love the connection. We want to see two people together happily ever after (or at least till the end of the movie). Why? Because we don't want to be alone.

We all want to do relationships right. We all want the dream of finding someone to be "the love of our life." But just walk down the halls at your school and see the drama unfold as people use people and then get discarded to the side—the way we're doing it now isn't working.

You want more than that. You want to do relationships right, in a way that's 180 degrees different than the way most people in the movies, in music, and in the halls of your school are relating to one another.

You want to find a way to get to know someone that's in line with the 180 God's doing in your life. You want to bring what God's done in your heart into what happens when you're with someone of the opposite sex—a way that keeps your heart and mind in check.

But before you can live out this 180, you have to grasp an important element of sex: it's selfless. What you think about sex and how you live it out isn't just about you.

That's a real 180 from the way the rest of our culture does sex. In movies, music, TV shows, or just the couples or hookups you see in your school, it's all about what another person can do for you—how they can make you feel or what they can do to bring you pleasure. People are used as tools for our own benefit with little regard for their humanity.

You can view sex as sacred, realizing there's something mysterious and holy about it. You can start taking sex seriously, realizing that even hookups leave a piece of you behind. You can let those beliefs transform you inside as you seek to live out the IOU—a life of inward character, outward modesty, and upward devotion.

You can see how there's a better way to do relationships than the fairy tales the rest of the world is trying to live out.

But sex isn't just a personal issue or a personal choice—it's not that simple. How you view sex and sexuality impacts others. It's not just your body and your decision. When you start interacting with someone else, you're responsible for both your actions and theirs. First Thessalonians 4:3–7 says:

> It is God's will that you should be sanctified: that you should avoid sexual immorality; that each of you should learn to control his own body in a way that is holy and honorable, not in passionate lust like the heathen, who do not know God; and that in this matter no one should wrong his brother or take advantage of him. The Lord will punish men for all such sins,

the revolution: one + one

as we have already told you and warned you. For God did not call us to be impure, but to live a holy life.

Reread verse 6: "No one should wrong his brother or take advantage of him." Even if the other person is a willing participant in a sexual act, there's some part of it that both people have to own up to.

For example, if you know someone's weakness and take advantage of it, you're arousing desires in that person solely for your own personal gain. Guys use it to get girls to give them oral sex. They see a girl who's insecure and is afraid of losing the relationship, so they figure if they can't pressure her to go all the way, they can at least make sure they get something from her.

Girls work it too—getting their needs met by taking advantage of how guys are wired visually by dressing in ways that make sure they are not only noticed but desired.

So if you really want to live in a way that's 180 degrees different than the rest of the world, how do you walk this out in your relationships? How do you honor God while keeping your heart and hormones in check?

How do you follow the relationship 180 we just talked about, keeping the spiritual, emotional, and physical all in the best order to make sure that you don't get massacred or maim someone else in a relationship?

How do you not only think differently about sex and attract the opposite sex differently—how do you also relate to the opposite sex differently?

> **How do you honor God while keeping your heart and hormones in check?**

[disconnecting the friendship]

Here's how most Christians do it.

Guy likes girl. Girl likes guy. They go out. Have a great time. Go out again. Become a couple.

And here's where things start getting really weird. They start treating each other differently. The friendship dies down. They start acting like they think a couple should act—and they take their cues no longer from their faith but from our culture.

What does this look like?

They put all their friendships on hold and become the center of each other's worlds.

They go on youth group trips but are oblivious to anyone else.

Mission trips are no longer about serving other people—they're pseudo-weekend getaways to "exotic" locales with 50 chaperones.

Church, Bible studies, and youth group become just another way they can see each other during the week.

They feel like they need to hold hands, kiss, make out—because that's what couples do, right? And the physical suddenly becomes a big deal between two people who previously enjoyed just hanging out.

It's like suddenly all the things they knew about being a good friend, about being a brother and sister in Christ, about encouraging the other person to grow—things that are part of their "regular" friendships in youth group or at school—don't apply anymore.

Wrong. They still do.

In fact, they're even more important now because when you continue to relate in those ways, your relationship looks very different than the way most people come together. And when you break up, the relationship also looks a lot different. Different is good.

Want to live out a sex180 in the way you relate to other people? Then start out as friends.

This shouldn't be that hard for some of you because a lot of people hang out with their friends anyway. Some people don't even date; they just go out with friends. But we're talking about real friends, the kind of friendships that impact your life in a huge way. And before we can move on, some of you are going to have to get past the f-word.

[the f-word]

"Friends? You've got to be kidding!" Some of you may be thinking, "That's not very romantic."

A lot of guys hate to hear the f-word, especially when it's thrown at them like this from an object of their affection: "I just want to be friends."

The reason is, it's often a cop-out. It's the nice way of saying, "I'm really not interested in you." And if you're romantically interested in someone, then the f-word is like a dagger in your heart.

If the whole "friends" thing sounds too boring for your romantic dreams, you may be suffering from what we call "the Bachelor/Bachelorette Syndrome."

Mike, a survivor of the Bachelor Syndrome, tells his story:

> I was in a relationship with a girl who was an extreme, hopeless romantic. She expected something romantic 24/7. I'm a very romantic guy, but it was really difficult to keep up with her expectations because I felt like I was always having to prove myself. I had to go beyond the normal. I had to think of something totally out of the ordinary because this girl had scenarios for every single thing. After a while, I failed. It was just so hard because I felt like our relationship was guided by what I could do to make this a romantic thing.

That's a huge amount of pressure, and it's a big example of the whole Hollywood way of interacting (for those of you with short-term memory problems, it was in the last chapter).

If you're going to start out as friends, you have to let go of the romantic and get past the Bachelor/Bachelorette Syndrome.

Even the greatest real love stories have moments that aren't so great. Even couples whose eyes dance every time they see each other have moments when they are completely blind to what the other person needs or is going through.

No one person is ever going to be all you want him or her to be. No one is always going to say the perfect thing. No one is always going to be there for you every moment you feel lonely or sad. No one is going to be totally and completely interested in your day, your life, your feelings, your thoughts, your dreams—no one but Jesus.

You can search and search for that one perfect love, but you're looking for a myth. It's fiction. Sorry. Perfect love never was meant to be a human-to-human love. It's a love only God can give.

God understands our desire to try to find that perfect person to fill the hole in our hearts. One day Jesus was talking with a woman who had looked for love in all the wrong places. But instead of rejecting her, he offered her the relationship and love she had desperately been looking for in a lot of broken relationships. Just like in the Hollywood way of relationships, she was looking for the right guy.

John 4 lets us in on this encounter Jesus had in Samaria. While Jesus was resting beside a well, a woman came along, and Jesus asked her for a drink of water. After all, she had a bucket, and he was thirsty. But as Jesus always amazingly does, he saw not only his physical thirst but also this woman's thirsty soul.

He told her about living water that could quench her thirst. She thought he was talking about some kind of magic water. But Jesus was referring to something much more significant, water for a thirst she had been trying to quench in a lot of different relationships. Jesus said, "You don't have a husband—for you have had five husbands, and you aren't even married to the man you're living with now" (John 4:17 NLT). And he was dead on. He knew. She knew. And she began to see that

the revolution: one + one

nothing she had been doing was alleviating her thirst—it was still there.

But she drank from the living water that Jesus offered her— water for her soul. She walked away from the well that day changed and no longer thirsty. She told those around her, "Come and meet a man who told me everything I ever did! Can this be the Messiah?" (John 4:29 NLT).

Girls, you have to lay down your chick flick dreams of the perfect romance.

Guys, you have to let go of your desire to be the center of one person's world.

If you surrender yourself and your expectations to God, you will avoid raising your expectations of a single person to a point where they are completely unrealistic. You'll also keep the relationship from fast-forwarding to much further along than it needs to be.

> **Promise me . . . not to awaken love until the time is right.**
>
> —Song of Songs 3:5 NLT

The Bible says "not to awaken love until the time is right" (Song of Songs 3:5 NLT). If you're going to do relationships God's way, if you're going to live out a sex180 in the way that you think and live out your sexuality, you're going to have to take it slow.

You're going to have to use your brain—not exactly a very romantic organ, but you're going to have to think it through. You can't just get caught up in the moment. You can't follow wherever your heart leads. Love, as we learned in the relationships180 chapter, requires work on your part. Sometimes it requires making a conscious decision to love. It's not all fireworks, kisses in the rain, or running across fields to embrace. True love requires sacrifice—and that makes love as strong as it is sweet.

So whether you're all about courting or dating or whatever, pace yourself. Let the friendship come first so you can really get to know someone and find out where their heart and priorities are.

Let's walk back through the steps of a relationship from the last chapter. (Notice we put them in the God's 180 way order—not Hollywood's.)

If you're attracted to someone you want to get to know better, then before there's even a hint of a romantic relationship, you need to learn as much as you can about the person. You need to know what they believe about God, and you need to be a part of their life to see if their actions back up what their mouth says. You need to see them in good and bad situations—and how they handle victories, defeats, and just the junk life throws at us. You need to find out who their friends are, see what their family is like, and observe how this person treats those closest to them.

All of that needs to happen before the emotions kick in. Yeah, those emotions may be lurking beneath the surface, but they're never acted on until you've lived out the friendship and seen the spiritual, psychological, and social in action.

That's why the word *friend* doesn't have to be the end of the world. It's not a cop-out. It's a beginning. In fact, it's the best way to guard your heart and someone else's.

[friends with benefits]

So what does this friendship look like? Is it real or just a pseudo-friendship where you're biding your time until you get the all clear on the boyfriend/girlfriend thing?

the revolution: one + one

"friends with benefits"

"Being in a relationship just complicates everything. You feel obligated to be all, like, couply. And that gets really boring after a while. When you're friends with benefits, you go over, hook up, then play video games or something. It rocks."—Brian, age 16[1]

Friendship means helping each other out, right? Giving each other what you need or want, right? Yeah, you're right—to a point. But friendship doesn't mean using someone as a tool to relieve your sexual tension, and that's what the whole friends with benefits thing is—a way to get some immediate satisfaction by hooking up with a buddy of the opposite sex for purely physical reasons. No emotions. No promises. Just sex.

Yeah, right. Sex isn't just physical. You can't dissect it like that, cutting away the spiritual and emotional connections. And even if everyone agrees up front that it's just about the sex, nothing more, the truth eventually surfaces.

Emotions will surface. Someone will feel a connection and want the relationship to be more than just a random, one-time thing. It's not because one person is weak. It's not because someone's too needy. It's because that's the nature of sex. It's how God created it to be. Sex is too sacred, too serious, and too selfless to be thrown around like that.

And honestly, how real is a friendship when it's all about how one person can use another? Would you settle for that in any other area of your life? Would you be okay with being used for your money, your smarts, or your car? No way. You wouldn't take it. You would say, "No thanks," and walk away.

Don't settle for poser friendships. Hold out for real friends and friendships that will respect not only you but what God says about how we should treat each other—selflessly.

If it is, then you're missing out. Because this whole friendship thing not only keeps a relationship at a good pace, it also has a lot of real benefits. (And we're not talking about hooking up with buddies just to have sex. See the sidebar.)

real friends, real benefits

Jesus said: "Greater love has no one than this, that he lay down his life for his friends" (John 15:13). And that's exactly what you have to do to make sure you live in a revolutionary way.

First and foremost, you have to say to yourself, "I'm going to relate to this person as a friend. I might have some feelings for her. But I'm not going there yet."

Theresa and I (Chip) were friends for about a year and a half before we became romantically involved. Although I was physically attracted to her the first time we met, I willfully chose to not go down that road. I had learned the hard way that I needed to get to know what was on the inside before I let my emotions or our relationship move beyond friendship.

When you start off with romance, you can rarely go back and establish a true friendship.

We were part of a larger circle of Christian friends. As friends, I wasn't trying to impress her or always trying to look my best. We weren't playing friendship as a game—we really were friends. We prayed together, shared together, worshiped together, and participated in ministry together. We learned an amazing amount about each other without the constant reminder that she was a woman and I was a man. Because we were part of a larger group, spending time together rarely involved being alone. Looking back, I realize that because our focus was on Christ and helping each other grow in him, I wasn't really aware of the way we were gradually being drawn together.

Friendship provides a great way to get to know other people without having to move on to romance. But when you start off with romance, you can rarely go back and establish a true friendship.

"Some teens use the excuse, 'Well, I really need to be in a relationship in high school because I need to practice for the future,'" said Annie, a high school senior. "But I think a huge argument for being friends is that you can relate to the opposite sex so much more, almost on a deeper emotional level,

the revolution: one + one

without messing around with physical stuff. You don't need something else to build your friendship on. I'm learning to relate to the opposite sex. It's fun and it's pure and it's holy. It's giving me so much practice for the future, whether we're boyfriend and girlfriend or not. Right now I'm just learning to communicate, and it's good."

The kind of friendship we're talking about isn't a passive, "whatever" kind of relationship where you're just hanging around someone, waiting for God to write on the wall that you should date. No, this friendship is driven by a very real desire to get to know someone, to see who they are beyond how great they look or how attractive they are to you. It's an active friendship.

So what does a real guy/girl friendship look like? Here are some ways to help you build a healthy and legit friendship.

Real friendships don't revolve around just one person. Have you ever had a clingy friend? Someone you enjoyed being with but was very high-maintenance? You felt like this person's whole life depended on you being there to help him or her through the next crisis. After a while, the friendship became a burden. It's not that you didn't want to help out anymore, but you just felt like anytime you did, the life was being sucked out of you. Every moment required more than you could give, and even when you gave your all, it just wasn't enough.

To have a healthy guy/girl friendship, you need other friendships too. Guys need buddies and girls need girlfriends. You need to know that you're not the center of someone's world. As ego-rich as that setup is, after a while that kind of friendship will drain you, not feed you. You need a friend who doesn't see you as the source of their happiness but sees God as that source. Someone who appreciates each relationship for what it is and doesn't come with a long list of expectations and needs because he or she is taking those to God first.

If God chooses to meet those needs through your guy/girl friendship, then that's awesome. But that doesn't make the friend your god. It makes your friend a reflection of God, a way he expresses his love for you.

A student named Bo says it this way: "God doesn't always show his love for us directly; sometimes he goes through other people. You can think of it as God loving them through you. In a relationship, you can feel God's love through the other person."

In a guy/girl friendship, the two of you don't see each other as exclusive. You have other people around and healthy, active friendships that enrich your lives. And the balance of those relationships helps keep the guy/girl friendship in perspective. You aren't pushing the friendship forward because you expect the other person to be your one and only source of happiness.

Healthy friends don't demand a lot from each other. They sometimes ask a lot, but it's never demanded.

Plus, when you both share a mutual friend—Jesus—you have a lot more to talk about. You are able to share things with each other that people who don't know him just wouldn't understand.

You can both discuss how you met Jesus and what drew you to him. You can tell each other what he's doing in your lives. You can talk about all the new things you're learning about him. You can share how he's helped you through rough times. You can even discuss the things about him that you just don't understand.

Real friends create comfortable places where you can be yourself. Real friendships are not about playing games or wearing masks. The kind of people who are your closest and best friends are the people you can let down your guard and just be yourself with. If you're having a really bad day, you can tell them about it. If you're grumpy, sad, hyper, or all of the above in a 30-minute span . . . you may need to seek professional help—kidding! Your friend isn't constantly evaluating you based on how you act that day. He or she understands that all of us sometimes handle life well and sometimes don't. A real friend doesn't come with a lot of expectations for how you should act.

My wife, Jennifer, and I (Tim) are great friends. Even before we were dating, we just loved being around each other. Our relationship was on and off a lot—mainly because I wasn't ready to step up and be the man I was supposed to be. But even in the midst of our "breaks," we were still friends. We still enjoyed being around each other. We laughed. We sang (yes, we really did). We just liked hanging out and talking. Sometimes we messed up the order of things, getting a little too physical or emotional, but truthfully, everything always came back to the friendship. We just loved being around each other. I still love being around her. She's my best friend.

When you have a front row seat in someone's life, you see his or her faith in action (or inaction).

Real friends have a front row seat in our lives. In our culture, the word *Christian* has become more of a label than a lifestyle. There are a lot of "Christians" out there, but not many followers of Christ—people who are sold out daily to God and trying their best to pursue an active, growing relationship with God. When you have a front row seat in someone's life, you see his or her faith in action (or inaction).

We're not talking about being the judge of someone's faith, because only God can judge someone's heart. But Jesus did caution us about buying into people's "I'm a believer" lines and gave some guidelines to make sure that someone's life backed up what he or she is saying:

> Watch out for false prophets. They come to you in sheep's clothing, but inwardly they are ferocious wolves. By their fruit you will recognize them. Do people pick grapes from thornbushes, or figs from thistles? Likewise every good tree bears good fruit, but a bad tree bears bad fruit. A good tree cannot bear bad fruit,

and a bad tree cannot bear good fruit. Every tree that does not bear good fruit is cut down and thrown into the fire. Thus, by their fruit you will recognize them.

Matthew 7:15–20

So what's good fruit? Galatians 5:22–23 tells us that "the fruit of the Spirit is love, joy, peace, patience, kindness, goodness, faithfulness, gentleness and self-control."

While you're getting an up-close glimpse into someone's life, look for the fruit of the Spirit. See how love, peace, patience, and the rest are showing up in their life. It's external evidence of what the Holy Spirit is doing on the inside of their life and a good indicator of how active their faith really is. It will help you distinguish between a "Christian" and a follower of Christ to make sure you both have the same solid foundation and the same passion for pursuing a growing, thriving relationship with Jesus (see 2 Corinthians 6:14).

Real friends don't use each other. Some people attach themselves to others solely because of what the other person can do for them. Proverbs 19:6 says, "Many curry favor with a ruler, and everyone is the friend of a man who gives gifts." But real friendships aren't based solely on what the other person has to offer (reread Jesus's words about laying down your life in John 15:13).

Some people become friends because of the other person's social position: "If I'm seen with this person, people will notice me." Others position themselves in someone's life so they can get close to a crush: "I'll be your friend because you're friends with Mr. Oh-My-Gosh-He's-Gorgeous."

And other people use their friends just for the emotional and physical perks they can get out of the relationship. It's almost like the friendship becomes a rest stop until the next great love of your life comes along. You use the other person for companionship, emotional support, and sometimes just physical needs. You like to kiss, so you find someone who will kiss you. You like to hold hands, so you find someone who will hold your hand. You like to snuggle up to someone, so you find someone who will snuggle with you.

You may not go as far as having sex, but you're still buying into the whole friends with benefits lie. "We don't mean anything by all of this. But it's just part of making someone feel good, right?" Wrong. It's just as much about using each other for physical perks as hooking up is. You're playing them. You're adding stuff into the friendship that just complicates it and keeps it from being all it can be.

When I (Tim) was in college, a friend and I had an idea: since neither one of us was dating anyone, we would be each other's "valentine" for the day on Valentine's Day. Someone to do nice things for and someone to go out with. Someone to make the other feel special. No strings attached.

And that's how an annual tradition began for Beth and me. For the next three years, on February 14 we were each other's designated valentine. We always left the loophole that if either one of us was dating someone, then the deal was off—but that never happened.

It started out pretty small. The first two years we exchanged cards and small gifts. We saw each other and said "Happy Valentine's Day." But our senior year, I had the big idea to go all out. Beth and I were just friends with no romantic attachments, and we knew that at graduation we would go our separate ways. So we decided to make this the best Valentine's Day ever because we had no idea when either of us would have a decent one again.

That morning I got up early and went and sang outside Beth's window. I bought flowers. I stood outside one of her classes with a big posterboard that read, "Happy Valentine's Day, Beth." I bought her a bunch of gifts. Stuffed her campus mailbox with notes. And that night, we went out to a nice dinner and a movie. I was so proud of how special I had made

Beth feel. And for many years, I looked back on that one day as a great memory.

That is, until I met Jennifer, my wife. Valentine's Day with Jennifer was different. It was more than having someone fill a blank spot in my life. It was more than just having someone to do nice things for. It was realizing that love isn't just romance; it's honoring the other person. Love is thinking about someone beyond what you get out of it—and the other person doing the same.

> **Love is thinking about someone beyond what you get out of it—and the other person doing the same.**

I did lots of nice things for Beth, but I didn't honor her. I didn't do anything physically immoral, but I sure did play games with Beth's emotions. Even though we both knew our relationship was only for one day, I made her feel special not because I thought she was but because of how great she would think I was. I lavished attention on her on Valentine's Day not because she needed it but because I did.

Beth was a friend—and only a friend. But I didn't treat her very much like a friend. We just used each other. Looking back, that Valentine's Day from college wasn't as great as it seemed. Oh, sure, I was in love. Unfortunately, I was just in love with myself.

What about you? Who are you really in love with—yourself? The idea of being in love? What's your real motive behind why you treat people the way you do?

Real friends use words wisely. A good friend cares enough to say things that are not always easy to say—but that you sometimes need to hear. Proverbs 27:6 says: "Wounds from a friend can be trusted, but an enemy multiplies kisses." Sometimes the things that are toughest to say are the things we need to hear the most. If you're acting like a jerk, sometimes you need someone to let you know you're acting like a jerk. If you're being too me-centered, you need someone to remind you that the world doesn't revolve around you. A friend who is brave enough and cares enough to speak that

the revolution: one + one

kind of truth to you is definitely the kind of person you want to keep around.

But a good friend is not only someone who will care enough to sometimes say the things we don't want to hear but also someone who cares enough to be careful about the words he or she does say. Let us give you an example.

Guys speak carelessly a lot with girls—and most of the time they are completely clueless about it. With their friends who are girls, some guys say things like "I want to marry someone like you someday" or even "I love you" without realizing the huge impact those statements have on a lot of girls. Guys think they're just attaching words to the warm feelings they have. They may even think they are throwing out a compliment. But a girl hears and processes those in a very different way than the guy may or may not have intended—it's just how she's wired. She hears, "I want to marry you," and "You are the love of my life." And to a girl, those words can feed that dream of a romance that may not even exist. So guys, be conscious of the power of your words.

But girls, you also can guard your heart. You don't have to let statements like that kick your mind into overdrive where you're trying on his last name, daydreaming about the wedding, and picking out baby names. You can also dream your way into thinking a relationship is more serious than it is, which can cause you to justify blurring your physical boundaries. If a guy is saying things that make your emotions and thoughts soar out of control, call him on it. Explain how it affects you. If he's a good friend, he'll respect that.

When Jennifer and I (Tim) were dating, she told me never to talk about marriage until I was ready to get on one knee and ask her. She knew what those words would do to her if I spoke them, and she also knew that her heart didn't need to hear them unless I could back them up. It threw me off at first, but then I appreciated it because it definitely made me think twice about what I said—especially when my emotions kicked

real friends, real benefits

in and I wanted to express my love for her. I understood that I had to choose my words wisely because they had an effect on someone else. It wasn't just about me. And I knew that I could show more love for her by respecting that than by telling her what I felt my heart wanted to express before I could back it up with a ring and a promise.

Real friends are honest with each other—but there are boundaries. There are some places a guy or a girl doesn't need to go in a conversation. Proverbs 4:23 says: "Above all else, guard your heart, for it is the wellspring of life." One of the ways you do that is to be smart about who you tell what.

> **Above all else, guard your heart, for it is the wellspring of life.**
>
> —Proverbs 4:23

Guys, if you're struggling with lust, you definitely don't need to go into too much detail with a girl about it—use your buddies for that. Girls, if you lose your brain every time a certain guy comes around, he's probably not the best person to help you sort those feelings out. Call your girl friends for that.

Be honest, use words wisely, but know where your boundaries are.

Real friends are not defined by their friendships. Take some people out of their circle of friends and they wander around like a lost kid. They don't know what to do. But real friends aren't defined by their friendships. They seek their identity in something more stable—who they are in Jesus Christ. They don't base their whole self on what their friends think; they base who they are on what God thinks about them.

Here are just some of the things God says about you:

> I have redeemed you;
> I have summoned you by name; you are mine.
>
> Isaiah 43:1

I no longer call you servants, because a servant does not know his master's business. Instead, I have called you friends, for

the revolution: one + one

everything that I learned from my Father I have made known to you. You did not choose me, but I chose you.

John 15:15–16

Your group of friends may change. Your wealth or social status may change. Your school may change. But who God says you are doesn't change.

Your friends are a big part of your life, but they're not all you're about. You bring much more to the table than just who *they* are—a lot more. That's what God thinks.

[the revolution inside]

- We have talked about some characteristics of real friend-ships—but we bet you could think of a few more. What are some that we have missed? What are some things you value in a true friend?
- How real are your friendships with people of the opposite sex?
- How does the way you treat your boyfriend or girlfriend differ from the way you treat your other friends?
- What could you do to enjoy the friendship more with the opposite sex and play down the romance factor?
- How can you live out the ways you know God wants you to view other people and yourself in your guy-girl friendships?
- If you've never had a real friend of the opposite sex and you want to learn how to be a friend to them, identify someone you have no romantic interest in but you really admire. Start taking some steps toward a non-romantic, non-sexual friendship. It's a safe place to start, and you'll be surprised how rewarding it can be to have a real friend who just happens to be a guy or a girl. If you're not sure

real friends, real benefits

how to do this, here are a few suggestions to get you started.

[hanging out with your friend]

If you think you might want to date someone but you want to make sure you maintain your friendship, go out as friends in a group. It will allow you to get to know someone without all the pressure of feeling like the success of a date is on your shoulders.

And if you find yourself one-on-one with someone of the opposite sex, stay focused. Use the moment as a relationship interview. Go to a place that allows you to talk. Keep the time together fun and light. Just be yourself and use the opportunity to find out more about who this person is, what he or she believes, and how much of a role God plays in his or her life.

Ask questions about his or her family, free time, faith, and spiritual growth. Sometimes it will help you put the whole crush thing in perspective when you see beyond all the outside package and get a glimpse of what this person is really like inside.

Starting as friends is a great way to live out the revolution. It's not as high profile as having someone on your arm to walk around school with, but it is definitely the best way to keep your heart—and someone else's—in check.

Going out doesn't change the way we should do relationships. The way you treat your friends also applies to how you treat those you date. Jesus said the two greatest commandments are to love God and love others (see Matthew 22:36–39). How a guy and girl who may be interested in each other act toward each other should be no different than the ways they encourage, build up, and help their friends. The things you do in your regular friendships apply to your relationship with a bf or gf too.

the revolution: one + one

There's also another way to relate to the opposite sex—a way that will definitely help you keep from "awakening love until the time is right" (see Song of Songs 3:5). It's a way that will help you continue to live out a sex180: treat each other like brothers and sisters.

Got that visual? Yeah, keep going. We'll explain.

Live out a sex180: treat each other like brothers and sisters.

real friends, real benefits

acting like you're related

9

One of the greatest friends I (Chip) have ever had in my life is my sister, Punkie. She is barely over a year older than me. In high school we took tons of classes together. I could talk to her about everything. Through Punkie I learned how girls think and why they do what they do. I saw in her life and in her character what I wanted in a girlfriend or mate someday. We talked, laughed, shared, and consoled one another through good times and bad. She came to know Christ in high school, and through her life I saw the difference between being religious and having a real relationship with Jesus.

Why do I share this? Because Tim and I have worked with and talked to thousands of teens and have learned that being friends is important, but we know an even deeper and more powerful way to relate to the opposite sex that will do way more than simply keep your hormones in check. It will teach you how to build the kind of relationship that we all long for. If you think becoming friends is radical, listen to what God says about how to treat the opposite sex:

> Do not rebuke an older man harshly, but exhort him as if he were your father. Treat **younger men as brothers**, older women as mothers, and **younger women as sisters, with absolute purity**.
>
> 1 Timothy 5:1–2

Aren't there some boundaries that almost automatically emerge if we treat each other as a brother or sister? I mean, think of how you treat your biological sister or brother.

Do you ever hug him or her? Of course.

Do you hug him or her like you hug some other people? Ewww. Of course not.

Do you ever express affection physically for a brother or sister in your family? Absolutely.

Are there certain places or ways that you would never touch your brother or sister? Yes!

Now that we've planted that image firmly in your mind and totally grossed you out, let's move on.

If you are a follower of Jesus Christ, you're part of God's family. First John 3:1 says, "How great is the love the Father has lavished on us, that we should be called children of God! And that is what we are!"

Like it or not, that girl or guy you're crushin' on is your brother or sister, spiritually speaking, of course (hopefully). Recognizing that reality can help you raise some serious walls in your relationship.

You can live out the sacredness and seriousness of sex. The friends thing? You may have gone that route before, and that's not a problem. But when you start thinking about the other person as your brother or sister in Christ—well, those are some revolutionary thoughts.

What if we said we're going to be friends first, and then, while being friends, said we're going to act like we're related and treat one another like brothers and sisters? What would that look like?

the revolution: one + one

First, seeing each other as brother and sister means you back off the physical part of the relationship. Remember the stages in a relationship from chapter 7 (spiritual, psychological, social, emotional, physical)? When you start factoring in the family connection, suddenly the physical being last on the list doesn't seem like as big of a deal.

Sometimes you will want to express what you're feeling inside in some way other than a smile or a glance. But the bro/sis thing will slow things down.

Bobby had been dating a girl for about a week when a friend asked him if he and his girlfriend had kissed. Bobby was intentionally taking things slow to make sure he was living out what he believed. He said, "The way I see it, the faster, sooner, and farther you go, the harder it becomes to live pure. I want to make sure that whatever I do, my relationship isn't a physical one. I want the emotions and God to be there before any lips ever touch. So many Christians are like, 'There's nothing wrong with kissing on the first date.' Yeah, there is. It's like you're going down a hill—the faster you go, the quicker you fall."

The faster, sooner, and farther you go, the harder it becomes to live pure.

—Bobby

Second, seeing each other as brother and sister means you think twice about why you're doing what you're doing. It's not just about what you physically do (or don't do) with someone. It's also about getting honest about why you're doing it.

"I was in a relationship for about five months," Mike said. "It was a good relationship. We were both Christians. But the thing that I beat myself up about is that I moved way too fast. We didn't go any further than kissing, but I felt like our relationship was based on our kissing. We would get together and hang out, then there would be the period of kissing. I felt like I was having sex. I'm not saying I was literally having sex, but it just felt like I was turning my back on God."

So does that mean that Christians shouldn't kiss? It all depends. For Mike, kissing was a big deal. It was something that had become way too important to him. There was something about kissing in that relationship, in that situation, that he knew was wrong, and it was taking priority over obeying what he thought God wanted him to do.

He hadn't done the work of moving through the spiritual, psychological, social, and emotional stages. He was giving the physical too much priority. Even though he wasn't having sex, kissing was still messing up how he knew he should be handling this relationship.

"I felt like kissing was my idol, and it totally consumed the relationship," Mike continued. "It's what led to the end of us being together. I just felt like we were so far off from what a Christian relationship should be. I look back, and as the guy, I should have been the leader in the relationship. I should have been the one stepping up and guiding us in the direction we should be going. But I felt like I took it the other way and turned the relationship into idol worship."

Drawing physical lines is tough because not only is your body telling you one thing, but our culture backs it up. Relationships have all these stages, all these unspoken levels, and if you want to have a "real" relationship, you're supposed to go through those motions. First base, just friends, going out, dating—whatever the label, attached to it is usually some kind of list of physical actions that you're expected to be doing at that point.

But when you think of the other person as your brother or sister in Christ, you bring a whole new level of caution to the relationship—despite how innocent or acceptable the ways you want to express your affection may seem. You want to draw the physical boundaries much earlier and much bolder.

So what does it mean to live out this brother/sister thing? After all, just the thought of dating your brother or sister is enough to send most people into therapy!

the revolution: one + one

not so great siblings

Amnon was Tamar's half-brother. They shared the same dad, King David. Amnon fell in love with Tamar—actually it was more like lust. Second Samuel 13:2 says: "Amnon became frustrated to the point of illness on account of his sister Tamar, for she was a virgin, and it seemed impossible for him to do anything to her." Yeah, ewww.

But those family boundaries didn't stop Amnon. In fact, he developed a plan to "have" her. He asked Tamar to make him some bread at his home. When she arrived, he asked her to bring it to his bedroom. He had sent everyone away, and they were in the house alone.

When she took the bread to him, Amnon grabbed her and said, "Come to bed with me, my sister" (2 Samuel 13:11).

"'Don't, my brother!' she said to him. 'Don't force me. Such a thing should not be done in Israel! Don't do this wicked thing. What about me? Where could I get rid of my disgrace? And what about you? You would be like one of the wicked fools in Israel. Please speak to the king; he will not keep me from being married to you.' But he refused to listen to her, and since he was stronger than she, he raped her" (2 Samuel 13:12–14).

Amnon not only disrespected family boundaries and committed a vile and violent act, he also discarded Tamar's reputation and desires simply for his own personal pleasure. And then after he got what he wanted, he threw Tamar away. "Amnon hated her with intense hatred. In fact, he hated her more than he had loved her. Amnon said to her, 'Get up and get out!'" (2 Samuel 13:15).

Does anyone actually live this brother/sister idea out? Mike is trying. He said, "Before I think about getting into a relationship with a girl, I look at her spiritual life. I want her to be at a level and maturity in her faith where we can have that relationship. I think the biggest thing is for a girl to just be real—to be real in her faith in God. I've had dating relationships with girls, and I've had awesome brother/sister in Christ relationships. The dating relationships with the girls have been great, but the brother/sister in Christ relationships have been so much better. They have been guided by godly means. When it comes down to it, the Christian relationship is to build each other up.

"Right now at this time in our lives, we need to build our foundation for the future. I'm 17, and I haven't been through anything hard. During this time in our lives, we need to make sure our foundation is strong because there are going to be a lot of tests that come. We need to be fully rooted in our faith at a young age; it's going to be hard to get rooted later on. Before you can get into a relationship, you need to be rooted. That relationship, that brother/sister relationship in Christ, should make it stronger. I think it's an awesome thing if it's done right."

The apostle Paul would agree. Paul wrote to the church in Rome: "Be devoted to one another in brotherly love. Honor one another above yourselves" (Romans 12:10).

So how do you do it right? How do you keep the physical aspect of your relationship in check? How do you respect the natural brother/sister boundaries that God intends and not only enjoy each other's company but actually build each other up?

Think about how you would want someone to treat your brother or sister. How would you want someone to respect him or her? How would you want someone to see your sibling? How would you want someone to watch out for your brother or sister?

[respect my bro or sis]

Listen to pop princesses or watch their videos and see them talk about how guys are jerks and how they're going to use

the revolution: one + one

guys just as much as guys have used them. Or listen to rappers sing about all the girls they're going to have sex with.

Respecting the other person as a brother or sister means recognizing that this person is not an object or a play toy. He or she is a human being, someone God considers valuable—so valuable that he sent his Son to give his life for that person.

Psalm 8:3–6 says: "When I consider your heavens, the work of your fingers, the moon and the stars, which you have set in place, what is man that you are mindful of him, the son of man that you care for him? You made him a little lower than the heavenly beings and crowned him with glory and honor. You made him ruler over the works of your hands; you put everything under his feet."

God places great value on human life—our culture doesn't. Our culture thinks everyone has a price tag and everyone is an opportunity for our pleasure. We're disposable.

"In a relationship," says Annie, "it's not so self-focused. A guy might think, 'I really want to kiss her now,' but is that really benefiting the girl? Will that really help her out in the future? So many times in a relationship we want to do something right now because it's fulfilling or enjoyable for us. But how are our actions affecting someone else?"

God values humanity so much that he sent his Son in human form to give us a new way to be human, a new way to live as flesh and blood, guided by the Holy Spirit and God's Word, the Bible.

That brother or sister you've got your eye on is not just there for your amusement, ego boost, or personal fulfillment. He or she is a person with a background, a family. He or she is someone with dreams and goals.

What if we quit seeing people as objects and started seeing them as walking stories? People who have histories, memories, dreams, experiences, families, and friends.

When you see a hot guy walk into the room, you don't camp out on his looks. Instead, you find out about the person.

acting like you're related

When you see a hot girl walk into youth group, you find out her story and don't just settle for staring at the cover.

Living out a sex180, living out this revolution, forces you to see more of that story. It's why you start out as friends, and it's why you see each other as brother and sister. You put in the effort to understand where someone is spiritually, socially, mentally.

What if we quit seeing people as objects and started seeing them as walking stories? People who have histories, memories, dreams, experiences, families, and friends.

Why do you think dads always want to meet your date? It's because your dad wants to make sure that whoever you're going out with realizes you're part of a family. He or she needs to see you not just as someone to go out with but as a person with many different aspects to your life. (Not to mention that he wants your date to know that if you hurt his daughter or son, you're going to have to deal with him.)

Getting to know the family is also why courting is popular with some people. Spending time with someone you like and his or her family makes you think twice about your actions because you see how crossing physical lines would affect not only that person but also his or her entire family.

God wants to make sure that you know the guy or girl you're spending time with is part of a family—his family. He values him or her as much as he values you. And he wants you to treat that person with the same amount of respect that he wants you to be treated with.

[love their skills]

Just as you would want someone dating your brother or sister to respect them, you also would want that person to appreciate your sibling for who he or she really is.

the revolution: one + one

You would want to see your brother with someone who recognizes his skills and encourages him to use them.

You would want to see your sister with someone who sees her strengths and provides support.

You would want them to treat your sibling in a way that allowed them the ability to express themselves in the unique way God made them. Nothing controlling, manipulative, or possessive at all.

Not everyone is wired the same. People react in different ways. So if you want to respect someone for who they are, you need to take the time to get to know them and avoid the temptation to believe that he or she is exactly like you—because they're not.

Just look at your siblings. You live in the same house. You probably have the same parents. And yet how can two people who have so much in common be so different?

It's because we're not clones. We're each given a unique set of DNA. We each bear the fingerprint of a Creator. We may have things in common, but we also have a lot of differences.

Treating one another as a brother or sister in Christ means accepting those differences. It means respecting one another's strengths and weaknesses. It means encouraging one another to use the gifts and abilities God has entrusted to each of us. It means knowing each other beyond the outside shell.

Both Chip and I (Tim) have twin sons. His sons are grown. Mine are in preschool. My sons are identical twins. People usually look at them and merge them into one person called "the twins." But since I'm part of their family, their dad, I see them as individuals, not as "the twins."

I know who likes to talk a lot and who only talks when he has something to say.

I know who is fearless and who holds back.

I know who eats whatever food is put in front of him and who would eat only peanut butter and jelly sandwiches if he was allowed.

acting like you're related

I know who likes to do things by himself and who likes to have people around all the time.

Because my sons are part of my family, I know things about them that people outside our family don't know. You can probably relate. You know things about your mom, dad, brother, or sister that other people don't—and they know things about you too! Most of the time, your family knows you very well.

Treating each other like brother and sister means respecting those differences and loving the other person simply because they're part of your family. Not because you have to, but because you share a common heritage with God as your Father!

[don't hurt 'em!]

Ever seen a big brother or sister in action? Not only do older siblings like to be in charge, but they also have a natural tendency to watch over younger brothers or sisters.

When you think about someone dating your brother or sister, you want someone who will not only respect him or her and see all the great things he or she has to offer but also keep your sibling out of harm.

Would you want your sister to date someone who abused her—physically or emotionally?

Would you want your brother to go out with someone who played games with him, flirting for a while and then dumping him after a couple of weeks?

Would you want your brother or sister to go out with a person who constantly pushed him or her to get more and more physical?

No matter how mad your brother or sister makes you, you wouldn't wish those scenarios on them!

Now, what about the object of your affection? If they were your brother or sister, how would you want someone to treat them?

the revolution: one + one

Guess what? If you're in a relationship with someone, you're in a position to act on that. You can make sure that the other person is protected.

First of all, you can protect the other person by getting a handle on your own emotions. If you go insanely jealous any time you see them talking to another person, you can control that. Not by trying to control them but by keeping your own heart in check. Just because you're in a relationship with someone doesn't mean you own them. That kind of jealousy is grounded in fear, and fear does ugly things to people. You can protect someone by not trying to control him or her.

If you tend to manipulate the other person to make sure the relationship is all about you—what you need, what you want to do, what you want to talk about—you can control that too. You can protect the other person from your manipulative games by remembering it's not all about you. Your mom and dad always told you to share with your brother or sister, and that means putting your needs on the back burner sometimes.

And when it comes to protecting the other person's purity (and yours), you can control that too. Especially guys. If you want to be a man, a real man, step up and lead.

In a marriage, guys are called to be the spiritual leaders of their home (see Ephesians 5:23). But guys, this isn't just a future, someday thing. You are training now for your future role. You can be a leader in your relationships now by stepping up and not putting your girl in a situation where you know you're both going to be tempted. Just like girls should help you out by watching what they wear, you can help a girl out by protecting her and not manipulating her through situations and emotions. Know when she's vulnerable. Know when you're vulnerable. And when the two of you are at those points—just stay away from each other.

When you both are weak, living out the sex180 becomes so much harder. Not impossible, but definitely more difficult. Audrey has found this true in her relationship. She tries hard

acting like you're related

to make sure she doesn't cross the physical boundaries she and her boyfriend have set up. But they both struggle with staying focused on God's sex180 way.

Audrey says: "When a boyfriend and a girlfriend are out alone, I feel like the boy is the spiritual leader. The guy should pray about it and should pray about not putting themselves in tempting situations. That's when it's the most difficult—when you're alone or you're anywhere you can be horizontal or anything like that. Boys are weak, and girls are weak too. You can't really say one is stronger than the other, because when it gets down to it and you're lost in the moment, it's tough. It's really hard to say no. It's more about not putting yourself in those situations and the boy not being selfish."

Recognizing and honoring the family bonds that we have in Christ can raise some significant protective walls in relationships. Seeing another person in the context of their bigger story—their individuality, their family, their skills—helps us see the object of our affection less as an object and more as another human being.

[the revolution inside]

- How would you want someone to treat your brother or sister?
- What ways could someone show honor and respect to your brother or sister?
- What would you have done differently in some of your past relationships if you had seen the other person as your brother or sister?
- What could you do differently in your current relationships to treat the other person as a brother or sister?
- What would it take for you to start living this out? What is holding you back? If something specific comes to mind, ask God to help you with that hurdle.

With both the friendship and the family ties established in your relationship, you're ready to live out the third and final revolutionary way of relating to one another.

[wait a minute!]

We've thrown out a lot of things to think about. And as you read through the friends and brother/sister stuff, you might have been thinking, "This is interesting, but honestly this isn't the way the world—or my world—works." But that's exactly the point!

We're talking about becoming purposely countercultural. Let go of the way our culture says to do relationships. Put it down and walk away.

If you're a follower of Christ, you're called to live your life in a radically different way than how the world normally operates. You're called to love enemies. Forgive people who hurt you. Believe in the unseen. Think of others before yourself.

First Peter 2:11–12 says you're no longer wired like the rest of the world: "Dear friends, I urge you, as aliens and strangers in the world, to abstain from sinful desires, which war against your soul. Live such good lives among the pagans that, though they accuse you of doing wrong, they may see your good deeds and glorify God on the day he visits us."

People aren't always going to understand why you do what you do. At times you're going to feel like an alien—not the extraterrestrial, "take me to your leader" kind but the living in a foreign country kind. You're going to feel like you don't fit in with the culture, you don't know the language, and you sure don't understand all the customs.

> **Be purposely countercultural. Let go of the way our culture says to do relationships. Put it down and walk away.**

acting like you're related

Don't let that hold you back. Just because you live here in this culture, in this world, doesn't mean you have to live like everyone else. If you know a better way to do things, then do it. That's what living the revolution, living a sex180, is all about.

Start out as friends, real friends. Treat each other like a brother or sister. And the final way to be revolutionary is to help each other grow spiritually.

We're not talking superficial "God talk" or simply going to church or youth group together. We're talking about a revolutionary, authentic relationship that causes the other person to look back three to five years from now and say, "Wow, I got so much closer to Jesus because of that person." So how do you do that? Keep reading!

the revolution: one + one

getting (and giving) something out of it

Breakups can be brutal. You have the awkward meetings in the hall at school. Friends who have taken sides. Whispers about who's at fault. Regrets about who did what. And sometimes you just feel used and stupid.

But what if breakups didn't have to be so devastating?

What if the person you went out with walked away from a relationship actually happy that the other person was a part of his or her life? What if somehow he or she had grown in their faith instead of growing bitter? What if somehow this person understood love more instead of wanting to never love anyone again?

What if someone's relationship with Jesus Christ was better after having a relationship with you?

Imagine if instead of walking away with regrets and emotional scars, someone walked away from the relationship looking more like Jesus Christ in some area of his or her life because of you. He or she loved God more. Grew more. Served more. Trusted him more. Learned more about him.

You've got the friends thing down. The friendship is established. You're making a real effort to get to know someone. Not an "I'm your friend who's secretly crushin' on you the whole time and just wants to be near you" friend. But a friendship that's authentic, active, and growing. A friendship where you see beyond how hot someone is and get to know the real person. A friendship where you see if the things that you're trying to live out—that sex is sacred and serious and that you want to be a person of inward character, outward modesty, and upward devotion—are also the goals of the object of your affection.

In addition to the friendship, you realize that this person is your brother or sister in Christ. You set up the normal physical boundaries that should be there between family members, and you treat him or her in a way that you would want someone to treat your brother or sister (assuming you actually like your siblings—if you don't like your brother or sister, well, that's another book).

But what if, in addition to the friendship and the sibling connection, you made the spiritual growth of the other person your top priority? What if you did relationships in such a way that your faith wasn't put on hold when you were with someone but instead it was kicked up a notch? What if you were actually seeking God more and learning more about him because of this other person?

It can be done.

I (Chip) am seeing it lived out in my own house. I have a beautiful 17-year-old daughter who has learned how to make Christ the center of her relationship with a quality, Christian guy. They amaze me as they memorize Scripture together, play guitar, and talk on the phone about what God is teaching them. They're also involved in ministry together at their school.

So how do you get a relationship like that? Read Hebrews 10:24–25: "Let us consider how we may spur one another on toward love and good deeds. Let us not give up meeting to-

the revolution: one + one

gether, as some are in the habit of doing, but let us encourage one another."

In this verse are three key components to making the spiritual growth of those around you a top priority in your life.

[#1: spurring one another on]

"Let us consider how we may spur one another on toward love and good deeds" (Hebrews 10:24).

Spurred anyone lately? It's not quite as painful as it sounds. Instead of thinking sharp, spiky things on a cowboy's boot, think more of pushing someone along. Giving him or her a boost.

Spurring someone on toward love and good deeds means building them up to live in ways that let the love of Jesus Christ shine through them. The apostle Paul was very good at this, constantly challenging, encouraging, and helping grow those around him.

Paul had a burning desire to see others grow. He wrote, "This is my prayer: that your love may abound more and more in knowledge and depth of insight, so that you may be able to discern what is best and may be pure and blameless until the day of Christ" (Philippians 1:9–10).

He prayed for others out of the depth of his heart: "I pray that out of his glorious riches he may strengthen you with power through his Spirit in your inner being, so that Christ may dwell in your hearts through faith. And I pray that you, being rooted and established in love, may have power, together with all the saints, to grasp how wide and long and high and deep is the love of Christ, and to know this love that surpasses knowledge—that you may be filled to the measure of all the fullness of God" (Ephesians 3:16–19).

Spurring someone on toward love and good deeds means building them up to live in ways that let the love of Jesus Christ shine through them.

getting (and giving) something out of it

So how can you spur someone on toward growth?

Serve together. Nothing grows you spiritually like following Jesus's lead and serving others. Encourage those around you to join you in rolling up your sleeves, sacrificing your time and schedule, and getting face-to-face with those in need. You'll be amazed at what you'll learn.

Read together. Another way to spur one another on toward growth is to study the Bible together. As you read it through, don't try to apply every verse to your relationship, because if you do that, you'll miss out. Read the Bible to discover who God is, who we are, and how we should live out our response to who God is in our lives. Also read the Bible on your own. You can help someone grow simply by letting God's words seep into your life and affect how you live.

Pray for each other. Pray for the other person to grow spiritually. Ask him or her specifically how you can pray. Beyond the "God, fix this" list, ask the person what specifically they would like to see God do in their lives and how they would like to grow closer to him. Then don't just say you'll pray and forget about it. Do it.

Here's something to keep in mind: when you're encouraging someone to grow, at times you will see some sparks. The Bible says, "As iron sharpens iron, so one man sharpens another" (Proverbs 27:17). When metal hits metal, there's some resistance. People are going to have some areas in their lives (just like you have in your own) where they may prefer God to take a "hands off" approach. Maybe it's a wound that's deep and hurts too much to even go there. Maybe it's a trust issue—"God, you didn't do what I thought you would before, so I'm not going to trust you with this part of my life." Maybe it's a sin issue, something they love more than God right now and are just not willing to give up for him.

At some point you've done all you can to point someone in the right direction, and he or she has to take steps of their own. Continue to encourage them. Continue to pray for them.

the revolution: one + one

But realize that God gives all of us the freedom to choose his best—or not. You can love your friends. You can encourage them. You can try to protect them. But ultimately, they make their own choices—just as you make your own. And watching how someone you know responds to that kind of conviction can be a huge insight into whether or not there's a future romantic angle to your relationship.

[tripping someone up]

While you're working hard to make sure that the people around you are growing spiritually, take a look at your own life to make sure nothing in the way you live, act, or talk could be tripping up someone else.

Jesus has some strong words to say to people who are so all about themselves that they are oblivious to how what they're doing affects someone else: "How terrible it will be for anyone who causes others to sin. Temptation to do wrong is inevitable, but how terrible it will be for the person who does the tempting" (Matthew 18:7 NLT).

Jesus didn't hesitate to hold people responsible for their impact on other people's lives. Do you realize how often our attitudes can cause other believers to stumble? Tripping someone up isn't just about having sex with another person. The things we laugh at, what we watch, what we pay money for, how we dress as believers in Christ all shout things much louder than our own personal declarations of the seriousness and sacredness of sex.

When you're disconnected, your heart and your life don't line up. People notice that. It trips them up. When our words and actions contradict each other, what we actually *do* matters more. It's what people see, and it's how people judge (accurately or inaccurately) whether we really believe this stuff we say and think.

getting (and giving) something out of it

When your life is disconnected, when your beliefs and actions aren't lined up, you become like the people God described in Isaiah 29:13. God said, "These people come near to me with their mouth and honor me with their lips, but their hearts are far from me. Their worship of me is made up only of rules taught by men."

This is the part where you back up what you say. You don't just mouth it; you bring it.

Sex isn't just your responsibility. It's not just a personal issue. What you do and think about sex affects not only you but everyone around you. And you have to be careful that you don't throw something in someone else's path that would trip them up.

Like what?

Trippin' over your outfit. We talked about modesty as a personal choice, about it being something you do to reflect how you desire to live out this sex180. But your choice of clothing isn't just about what you decide to wear. What you put on can cause someone else to stumble in his or her efforts to live purely.

What you do and think about sex affects not only you but everyone around you.

"Sounds like a personal problem to me," you might be thinking. "A girl or a guy should be able to dress any way they want, because if the other person lusts, that's their choice." True, a person chooses to entertain those thoughts—but you don't have to feed them.

We've talked enough about this. Listen to some others, people who walk the halls of high school every day.

MIKE: Guys are wired physically, and it's a bummer because every single time we see a girl dressed in skimpy clothes, it totally distorts our image of a woman of God. It's so hard to see not only the non-Christian but a lot of the Christian girls that are seriously killing us guys with lust. With my accountability group, we talk about the main

the revolution: one + one

things that pull us away from God. Every week we have a set of questions like "How are you doing in this area?" And I don't have to bring up lust because I know that's something every guy struggles with. It's almost like girls are holding up signs, "Here, see me and I'll pull you away from God."

AUDREY: When my boyfriend and I first started going out, he would tell me, "Audrey, you can't wear that with me." I wasn't offended at all. I was taken aback, but I was so thankful he told me that. I was like, "Okay, I'll go change." It was good.

AMY: I've never had a guy tell me, "I don't like it when you wear low-cut shirts." The response that girls get when they wear that kind of stuff is that guys like it because you get more attention. And sometimes we might think we're being modest, but we don't always know. One day I asked my friend, "Is this modest?" I didn't know where I should draw the line.

ANNIE: There are days when I just get out of bed, no makeup, and go to school. And people say, "You look really pretty today." And I'm like, "Wow. I love it." It's really encouraging. Getting words of affirmation from guys is huge. We really need that—even if it's just from our brothers in Christ.

AMY: It's just nice when you had like five minutes to get ready and you know you look like crap. There's just like no hope. And somebody says, "You look real pretty," and I'm like, "What?" It's just real nice.

AUDREY: I was having a problem with my friends not really getting the message. I was talking to one of my guy friends about what to do and he said, "Maybe on days when she's wearing something modest, you say, 'You look really nice today. That's a really good outfit.' She'll realize what looks good on her."

getting (and giving) something out of it

Trippin' over someone's words. While some girls may wonder why they have to make some different choices just because guys have a problem with it, some guys will wonder why they can't just say anything they want, and if a girl has a problem with it, she can just get over it.

Just like a girl showing off her body by the way she dresses feeds guys' physical lust, the words a guy says can feed a girl's emotional lust. Guys are wired visually, but girls are motivated by relationship and connection. And just as a guy's hormones feed off visual stimulation, a girl feeds off things that stimulate her emotions.

> **Just like a girl showing off her body by the way she dresses feeds guys' physical lust, the words a guy says can feed a girl's emotional lust.**

If you're a guy who has a lot of girl friends (notice the space between those two words), you may be clueless about this. You have your girl who you hang around with, call up all the time, and share your dreams and frustrations with, yet when it comes to romance or attraction, she's not for you. But for the girl, you've just fed her a lot of the things she's looking for in a relationship—companionship, intimacy (emotional, not physical), and conversation.

We're not saying you can't be friends—but be careful. Make sure you're not feeding a romantic relationship unless you're willing to back it up with your own actions and a sacrificial love. First Corinthians 13:4 says, "Love cares more for others than for self" (Message).

A guy can create huge stumbling blocks in a girl's path and really throw off her walk with God. Guys who don't want to trip up girls with their words (or actions) care more about how what they do will affect others than their own need to do it.

Girls, if you're thinking you're off the hook here, think again. While guys aren't as words-driven as girls, there are still some ways that a girl can use a guy for companionship, all the

the revolution: one + one

while sending out subtle signals with her words and actions that keep a guy thinking "maybe" in the romance department. If you're always available to hang out, to listen, and to let him pay for everything, you're saying to the guy with your actions something that you may not want to say. And that can lead to a nasty fall for a guy.

Trippin' over the physical line. Something that may not seem like a big deal to you could be a huge deal to someone else. After Jesus's death and resurrection, when Christianity was spreading through the Jews and to the Gentiles, many of the Jews were offended by the Gentiles' eating habits—the Gentiles had no problem with eating pork. Now, Old Testament law had been clear about eating certain kinds of animals, and the Jews had a strict rule not to touch the other white meat. The Gentiles had never followed those rules and really didn't see what was the big deal with eating a few pork chops.

But it was a big deal because their choice to chow down on some bacon was causing others to stumble. So Paul wrote, "Do not destroy the work of God for the sake of food. . . . It is wrong for a man to eat anything that causes someone else to stumble" (Romans 14:20).

The same principle applies to entertainment, holding hands, kissing, whatever. If something is not clearly defined as a "no" in the Bible, you need to be honest with yourself about how those things affect you, realizing what you can and can't handle. Ask yourself, "How does this affect me spiritually? How does it affect my walk with God?" If something you're doing is pulling you away from loving God and loving other people, then back off and run the other direction. And if something someone else is doing is what's tripping you up, speak up and let the other person know.

Also, you need to rely on those friendship skills and ask those same questions about the other person: "Does this affect him or her spiritually? How does this affect his or her walk with God?" Some things you can do and not feel like it hinders your

getting (and giving) something out of it

walk with God. But what may not trip you up could cause another person to stumble.

Audrey found herself in a situation where she and her boyfriend had different opinions on where to draw the line physically. She said, "I've had many times where my boyfriend's left and I didn't think we were doing anything wrong at the time, but later I would just sob. I would be just like, 'Why am I so upset?' And it was because I couldn't be before God alone because of what I just did.

"He doesn't have to understand why I have certain boundaries. I don't have to explain to him in detail. Sometimes it's bad to talk about things in detail because it can excite you more than actually doing it. Sometimes I've said, 'We can't do this. I can't tell you why, I just can't do it. You're going to have to get over it.' That's something a guy has to understand. When a girl says no, that's no."

So where do you draw those lines? Find the point of the temptation, then move it back a few steps to make sure you don't even come close.

"My boyfriend and I sat down and made a list of over 20 rules of just things we shouldn't do. Things like we're not allowed to give each other full frontal hugs anymore," Audrey explains. "When you cross lines, you're like, 'How did we even get here?' But if you draw those lines back further, you don't even get there. We've broken the full frontal hugs just a few times, but if that's the worst we've done, we're doing good because I don't feel like that's taking me away from God. That's just a rule we set to keep us from getting anywhere close to anything happening."

[#2: not give up meeting]

"Let us not give up meeting together, as some are in the habit of doing" (Hebrews 10:25).

the revolution: one + one

Have you ever noticed how when some people couple up in your youth group, they drop out of sight for a while? It's like their spiritual life gets put on hold so they can work on their relationship. It's amazing how they can juggle a full schedule of classes and extracurricular activities, but somehow when it comes to faith and their relationship, they can't multitask.

We're not saying everyone does this. In fact, some people really encourage each other to stay plugged into church, even challenging each other to pursue God more. And that's a great thing.

But for others, either they both disappear or one puts their faith on hold and attempts to let the other one drag them around spiritually. It's almost like they say, "Okay, you follow Jesus, and I'll follow you."

That's dangerous—not to mention you just took God out of the top spot in your life and put someone else in it. God doesn't want a secondhand relationship with you. Imagine this:

"Would you tell Kelly I love her?" God asks Ryan.
"God says he loves you, Kelly," Ryan tells Kelly.
"Would you tell God that I think he's great too?" Kelly asks Ryan.
"Kelly thinks you're great too," Ryan tells God.
"Would you tell . . ."

Don't you just want to scream out, "Stop it! Talk to him yourself!"? That's what God wants. He wants a direct connection with you, not a three-way call.

Jesus's death and resurrection restored a relationship between us and God—a relationship that was severed by humanity's sin in the Garden of Eden. God is holy. We are sinful. Sin and holiness don't go together—at all. So something had to be done in order for sin and holiness to be in the same room.

Jesus, who is holy, took on the sin of humanity so that we could come into God's presence and have a relationship with

getting (and giving) something out of it

him. So that we could talk with him. So that we could have an active, day-to-day friendship with him. So that his Spirit could live in us and help us not only understand how to live like him but also understand his Word, the Bible.

A huge price was paid so that we could have a direct connect with God. God didn't do all of that to guilt you into talking with him. He wants to talk to you—just as much as you want to talk to your friends every day. He wants to be a part of your life. He wants you to tell him about your day. He wants you to come to him for guidance, direction, or just comfort.

When your crush starts crushin' your time with God (and you start crushing theirs), you need to step back.

So when your crush starts crushin' your time with God (and you start crushing theirs), you need to step back. Don't let them give up on their meeting with God or other believers. You're not their God. You don't complete your bf/gf, and he or she doesn't complete you. The only way you two are going to have a healthy relationship is by both actively seeking God on your own in individual, personal relationships with God.

Sometimes you don't even realize you're shortchanging God. Amy and Bo, who had been dating for a few months, both saw that they were getting off track.

"I think that I've been basing my happiness off of Bo," Amy said. "I realized I was doing that when I saw how I was spending more time with him than God. I would stay on the phone till 11 p.m., then try to have some time with God. I would go through the motions, reading my Bible, then falling asleep while I'm praying. I was getting more out of my conversation with my boyfriend than I was with God—and that's so wrong. I would say that our relationship is God-centered, but it's starting to slip a little bit. I haven't really noticed, but it's been like that for a month. I started realizing it and it's getting back on track, but you need to find out if your relationship is God-centered or self-centered."

So what did Bo think about this?

the revolution: one + one

"When Amy told me that our relationship was straying from being God-centered, it was really something that was on my heart too," said Bo. "When she brought it up, I was like, 'You know, you're really right.' We talked until it was really late. When we got off the phone, I could have slacked off on my quiet time, but I didn't. 'Cause that's what I've been doing lately. But remembering that conversation helped me keep on my quiet time. Even today, I saw her for like an hour, but things just seem to be better now because God's really there."

Amy added, "When I told Bo that I felt like our relationship was slipping, I thought, *What if I say this and he gets mad?* But if our relationship is God-focused, speaking up is going to bring you or the relationship back. Don't be afraid to say it because God's going to work through that and make your relationship better."

Don't give up meeting with other Christians at church and at youth group, and especially, don't give up meeting with God. He wants that one-on-one time with you daily. Pursue that in your own life. But also encourage the other person in the relationship to do the same by creating time and space for it so that you help him or her grow spiritually.

Always wanting to be with someone and never allowing him or her time to do their own thing isn't what love is all about. It's insecure. It's actually kind of ugly. It's much more attractive when someone feels secure enough in who he or she is, and who the other person is, to allow some freedom in the relationship for each to pursue God on their own.

[#3: encouragement]

"Let us encourage one another" (Hebrews 10:25).

Your friends, your youth group, other Christ-followers who come into your path—what can you do to help them? What can you do to encourage them? Because let's face it, following Jesus Christ is hard sometimes! At some moments you want to

getting (and giving) something out of it

give up. Sometimes you want to walk away, you don't want to do the right thing. Sometimes you get so tired of being so different, so radical, and you just want to fit in.

But if we're going to be a part of a revolution, if we're going to live out this sex180 and launch a second sexual revolution, we're going to have a fight on our hands. Not against people but against lies. And at times it's going to get tough. So we need support from each other. We need to prop each other up, like Aaron and Hur did for Moses in the Old Testament:

> As long as Moses held up his hands, the Israelites were winning, but whenever he lowered his hands, the Amalekites were winning. When Moses' hands grew tired, [Aaron and Hur] took a stone and put it under him and he sat on it. Aaron and Hur held his hands up—one on one side, one on the other—so that his hands remained steady till sunset. So Joshua overcame the Amalekite army with the sword.
>
> Exodus 17:11–13

We get weary and we need encouragement. In fact, the Bible says that encouraging others is a daily part of keeping other believers on track. "Encourage one another daily, as long as it is called Today, so that none of you may be hardened by sin's deceitfulness" (Hebrews 3:13).

The Bible is really clear about telling people who love Jesus to encourage other people who love Jesus (read Romans 15:1–2 and 1 Thessalonians 5:11). So how do you do that?

Sometimes it's the words you say. You let the other person know that you see something in them that they may not be able to see right now. You let that person know how they have encouraged you in the past and what kind of contribution they have made to your life. You remind them of a promise from God or a verse that offers hope for their hopelessness. Proverbs 16:24 says, "Pleasant words are a honeycomb, sweet to the soul and healing to the bones."

the revolution: one + one

Sometimes it's what you don't say. James 1:19 says, "Everyone should be quick to listen." It's easy to find people who are eager to give their opinions on what we should or shouldn't do, but sometimes the most encouraging thing we can do is to keep our mouths shut and just listen. Sometimes we don't want a solution; we just want to know that someone cares and hears us.

Sometimes it's what you do. It's as simple as seeing a need in someone's life and doing something about it—either through your own resources or by finding someone who can help. Jesus said, "I was hungry and you gave me something to eat, I was thirsty and you gave me something to drink, I was a stranger and you invited me in, I needed clothes and you clothed me, I was sick and you looked after me, I was in prison and you came to visit me" (Matthew 25:35–36). When we reach out and encourage someone through our actions, we refresh their souls. We give them hope, and most of all we remind them that God loves them and he's watching over them.

[left behind]

Imagine a relationship with a person of the opposite sex in which you became good friends, treated each other as brother and sister, and wanted the other person to walk away, no matter what happened, saying, "You know what? Nothing romantic happened like I kind of secretly hoped, but because of my relationship with you, I'm more like Christ."

What if that was always the guiding principle in the revolution? You're going to build relationships, so build them so that whether it goes somewhere or not, the other person will say, "I was never defrauded. That person was a great friend. I learned a lot from my brother (or sister) in Christ, and because of them, I am more like Christ."

"Because of my relationship with you, I'm more like Christ." What if that was always the guiding principle in the revolution?

getting (and giving) something out of it

If you can live out these three revolutionary ways to relate to others, you're going to avoid all the games most people play. You're going to get the most out of your relationships. When you've made the friendship, brother/sister connection, and spiritual growth of someone else a priority, you've built a relationship on solid ground. It doesn't matter if it's dating or courtship—the principles transcend the labels.

Bobby knew all about the sex180—and he really wanted to live it out. So when he started dating Megan (not her real name), he was very intentional about what he did and didn't do.

He thought through the pyramid, the 180 way of doing relationships. He set up boundaries in the relationship and in his own head to keep the physical and emotional last on the list. He pursued the spiritual, psychological, and social so that he could really get to know who Megan was.

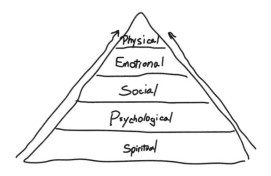

This wasn't because Bobby wasn't attracted to Megan. He definitely was. But he felt like the more physical they got, the more difficult it would be to see how truly compatible they were and also find out what Megan was all about. Bobby felt that the physical would become a kind of crutch and help them justify staying together longer than maybe they should.

They had a great time together, but after about a month, Bobby noticed that Megan wasn't quite on the same page as he was spiritually. Things that were a big deal to him—like reading the Bible and spending time with God every day—didn't

the revolution: one + one

seem to be as important to Megan. It's not that Megan wasn't a Christian; she was. But Bobby just didn't feel like they were compatible spiritually.

Even though they enjoyed each other's company, Bobby felt like the spiritual aspect was a significant enough difference that he should not pursue things any further. And it wasn't just Bobby; Megan also felt like the relationship had gone as far as it could. After two months of going out, they broke up. The two agreed to remain friends. And they actually did.

Because they had not been physical with each other, they didn't leave with a lot of regrets. They didn't have a lot of binding connections with each other. They both walked away with a friendship intact and the opportunity to get to know someone better.

So when you do relationships this way, does that mean breakups never hurt? No way. Honestly, no matter how much you try to keep everything in check, you are going to hit times when you wish or hope for something more. You're going to like the other person more than he or she likes you. You're going to think you're more compatible than the other person does.

But when you take it slow—start out as friends, treat each other like brother and sister, make the spiritual growth of the other person a priority—you see the relationship more clearly. You may not want to walk away at some point, but you'll definitely know when it's not only the right thing to do but also the right time to move on because you won't be foggy with emotions or physical hang-ups.

[the revolution inside]

- How can you make the spiritual growth of others a top priority?
- Who are some people in your life who need to be "built up"?

getting (and giving) something out of it

- What could you do to build them up this week?
- What are some things in your life that could be a potential stumbling block to others? What can you do to make sure that nothing trips them up?
- Who are some people in your life you can trust to call you out on the stumbling blocks in your life?
- If you are in a relationship with someone, how much time are you spending with that person in comparison with how much time you are spending with God?
- What specifically can you do today to make the spiritual growth of others a top priority when you are at school? At youth group? At home? At your job? On your team? In your club?

[you've got a question]

"That's awesome," you may be thinking. "I really want to build up others around me. I want to live out a real friendship. I want to see this person in my life as my brother/sister in Christ. But . . . well, I still have a few questions." We thought so. Is this what you're wanting to ask?

- What do we do when the romantic sparks happen? How do we know when it's time to pair off and test the relationship romantically in a God-honoring way?
- What about kissing—okay, or a wait-till-your-wedding-day thing?
- How do you know when you're more than friends?

the revolution: one + one

- How do you know if it's really love or just a crush or infatuation?
- We tried a relationship and it worked for a while, but now it's not so great. What do we do?

We're not going to leave you hanging—well, at least not more than the time it takes you to turn the page. (You can live with that, right?)

getting (and giving) something out of it

what abouts

Darren and Nichole have been friends since their sophomore year. Darren has had some very physical relationships in the past, but his sophomore year was a shift for him. After a nasty breakup with a girl he had been sexual with, Darren decided to back off all dating until he could figure out how to do this whole relationship thing right. So he took some time to get really focused on growing in his faith, and he's made a huge effort to make sure that his beliefs don't just show up at church but are seen by everyone else in his life.

Nichole has always been focused on doing a lot of service projects and has never really had time for a bf/gf relationship. She has lots of guy and girl friends and enjoys hanging out with them. She has a real passion for God and is always looking for ways to live that out.

They're in the same youth group. Nichole is part of an outreach team that tutors kids at a nearby apartment complex and often shares her faith with some children in very bad situations. Darren is on the baseball team at school and leads a Bible study with some of the guys from his team.

Nichole has watched Darren go through some tough times with the divorce of his parents and his brother's difficulty in dealing with the whole thing. She's been a great support to Darren, praying for him and offering well-timed encouragement.

They are great friends, but lately they've been wondering if there's something else. They've been having some "feelings" for each other, and they're not sure exactly what to do with them. They don't want to push something that may not be there. But then again, if something is there, they don't want to miss out on that either.

What do you do when you've lived out this revolution and now you have these emotions, these feelings for another person, and you just aren't sure what to do?

What do you do when you've lived out this revolution and now you have these emotions, these feelings for another person, and you just aren't sure what to do?

You know in your heart that sex is sacred and serious—and you live it out. You've made this revolution a priority in your own life by working on your inward character, outward modesty, and upward devotion.

You've decided to relate to the opposite sex not Hollywood's way but God's sex180 way. You see sex as selfless and that relationships are not all about you. You take your relationships slow. You put in the effort to get to know others. You start out as friends. See them as your brother or sister. And you make the spiritual growth of others a top priority.

You're living out the revolution. You walk through the process of getting to know the other person and respecting him or her. You find out the individual behind the great smile or body.

You may make some mistakes along the way; you may get some things out of order or be a little too focused in one area and not enough in another. But when you get off track, you stop, look where you are, make the necessary adjustments to your life, and jump back in.

the revolution: one + one

But what now? What if there's something else happening? How do you know what's next?

Here are some FAQs for those living out this sex180.

If I'm supposed to relate to the opposite sex as friends, treat them as a brother/sister, and be concerned with their spiritual growth, then how do I know when we're more than friends or brother/sister? The friendship doesn't have an expiration date, and neither does the brother/sister label. Just because you're interested in or attracted to someone doesn't mean that none of these truths apply anymore. Your girlfriend is still your sister in Christ. Your boyfriend is still your friend. And if you keep that in mind the whole time, you'll bring much more to each other's lives than just the fact that you have achieved coupledom or have someone to hang out with on the weekends. You're always friends. You're always brother and sister in Christ. And you should always be concerned that the other person is growing spiritually—even to the point of removing yourself from the relationship if you feel like that's the only way he or she can grow.

Then when can we date (or court, go out, or be a couple)? Before you ask us, you need to sit down and bring your parents into the loop. Share your heart. Share with them how you are doing relationships and why. Ask for their counsel and be willing to really listen to them. Even if that means they say "wait" on dating. Even if that means listening to some stuff that may be hard to hear—like their major concerns about you that they feel you need to address before they let you move on. You can't live all this out in obedience to God if you disregard the authorities God has placed in your life.

Ephesians 6:2–3 says, "'Honor your father and mother'— which is the first commandment with a promise—'that it may go well with you and that you may enjoy long life on the earth.'" If you want to get the most out of this revolution, if you want to not only live but get the best out of life, then part of living all of this out is obeying. And that obeying starts first with God. Then with your parents. Anything less will not "go well with you."

If your parents don't believe in Jesus Christ, does that mean you can skip this step? No way. In fact, God has just given you a huge opportunity for you to pass on all he's been teaching you. Let them know about the 180 God's been doing in your life. And if what they think about what you and your bf/gf should be doing doesn't line up to how God views relationships, then respect them, love them, but walk in obedience to God first.

If your parents don't believe in Jesus Christ, does that mean you can skip this step? No way.

Like we mentioned before, we don't have many great examples of this 180. The generations that have come before you have made a mess of relationships. Maybe you have a mom or dad who's on their third or fourth marriage. Maybe your mom spends more time online chatting with other men than she does talking to your dad. Maybe your dad has withdrawn from everyone in your family and seems to be looking for connections elsewhere. If that's your life (or close to it), your mom and/or dad may not be all that thrilled about what you're doing or even understand it. That's okay. Line up your life with what God says, respect your parents, and when they see that you're pursuing God's best while honoring their authority, they may start to do their own 180. You could be the example they need to find a better way to do relationships and think about their sexuality. Ironic, huh?

If you get the green light from your parents that you're ready to date, hold up one more minute. That doesn't necessarily mean you're completely ready to date. *You* need to make sure you're ready—that your heart, mind, and soul are ready for a relationship.

"When I'm in a relationship, I need to make sure I'm spiritually ready and spiritually mature," Mike says. "You can't go into a relationship without being spiritually toned in your

the revolution: one + one

walk. The best thing about not having that relationship in my life now is that I can focus all of my energy and all my time on my walk with God.

"I wouldn't be able to give the girl I'm dating enough of the time she needs or the spiritual growth that she needs because I'm swamped right now. I feel like there are seasons. There are seasons when you should be with someone from the opposite sex to help you grow. And there are seasons where you need to sit back and be like, 'Where am I at in my relationship with God? Am I pleased? If I'm not pleased, what can I do? What strategic things can I do to get myself to the level where I need to be at this point in my walk?'"

Amy and Bo agree. "Not everyone who has a boyfriend is going to be sexually impure," Amy says. "Having a boyfriend is not always a bad thing. I'm sure in some aspects it would be easier not to have a boyfriend, but it can also make your relationship with God stronger as you grow with the other person."

Bo adds, "Before my relationship with Amy, I wasn't motivated in my faith at all. I've really gotten to see inside her life, and I'm amazed by it. It's got me more motivated about God. I really didn't read much of the Bible. I wasn't really into it until I saw Amy's life and how it affected her."

Deciding to enter into a relationship is a matter of being honest enough with yourself to ask, "Will a relationship hinder my walk with God at this time, or am I grounded enough spiritually to handle it and handle the relationship in a revolutionary way?" If you're not sure, seek godly counsel from your parents, youth pastor, youth leader, and close friends. People whose spiritual lives are clearly on track. People who know you very well and will tell you the truth, not just what you want to hear. They may see some neediness in your life that needs to be brought to God and not brought on a date.

Annie offered these great questions to ask yourself to make sure you're ready for a relationship:

- Are you spending consistent time in God's Word?
- Are you becoming more like Christ daily?
- Are you consistent in your growth in the Lord?
- Are you involved in your church?
- Are you at a point where you can lead other people to Christ?

Audrey summed it up best: "I think the people who can handle relationships are the people who are fine without one—who are content without a boyfriend or any significant other."

So when is it okay to kiss someone? The physical should be last on your list. And by that we mean you should draw the line far away from anything sexual. Your view of relationships should be built first around the revolution of one and seeing sex as sacred and serious. You should be striving for inward character, outward modesty, and upward devotion. For some that may mean kissing is off limits. For others it may mean that it's okay.

But don't bring the physical into the relationship until you've walked through the other four stages—spiritual, psychological, social, and emotional. You need to know this person so well that you know where he or she stands on the whole kissing thing. If the other person thinks that a kiss is just something you do at the end of the date, then you definitely don't want to go there. But if the other person believes that a kiss is something that you had better back up with some true, God-centered love, not just infatuation, then that's okay.

Keep in mind that you don't want to trip anyone up in their walk with God. And remember that the more you bring the physical into the relationship now, the harder it is

> **The people who can handle relationships are the people who are fine without one—who are content without a boyfriend or any significant other.**
>
> —Audrey

to slow things down. The kind of kissing you do can really push things forward too. In other words, if you kiss, keep your mouth closed.

How do you know when someone is more than a buddy? How do you know when you're really in love? How can you tell if your love is true or if you've come down with a bad case of infatuation? How do you know the difference?

Take this quiz.[1] Read through each question to determine what's really going on beyond the rapid heartbeat and warm feelings. After reading each point, you should know whether you're in love or infatuated in that area. Write an *I* for infatuation next to each number if you think infatuation describes your relationship and an *L* if you think you're in love. (If you're someone who hates to write in books, grab a separate sheet of paper and write them down.)

When you're done, add up your *I*'s and *L*'s and take a look at your totals to see if you're crazy in love or just crazy.

_____ #1 Love takes time to grow. Infatuation explodes in an instant. You usually think, "Boom! I'm in love." Truthfully, we think someone should just delete the words "falling in love" from our vocabulary. You can fall into infatuation, you can fall into lust, but you usually grow into love. Love develops out of relationship and caring and core personal character traits, not our first impression of another person. We're wise not to declare love until a significant amount of time has passed. If some guy or girl says they're in love right away, they're not. They're infatuated.

Are you in a rush to label certain feelings "love," or do you have other words to describe those feelings? How much time do you think needs to pass before love can be clearly identified? If you find yourself "falling in love" often and early, only to be disappointed later, remember that loves takes time to grow—it will save you some heartache.

> The kind of kissing you do can really push things forward too.

what abouts

_____ **#2 Love grows out of knowing all that you can about the other person—good or bad.** Infatuation is happy to know very little about someone so it can leave the rest to the imagination. Infatuation lives in a make-believe world where the object of our affection is perfect, flawless, and completely devoted to us.

True love longs to know all about someone—the good, the bad, and the ugly. Love wants to study the other person's needs, dreams, and hopes because it wants to do everything possible to make them a reality. Infatuation quickly decides it knows everything it needs to know about someone.

_____ **#3 True love focuses on the other person. Infatuation is self-centered.** You know what infatuated people are all about? Themselves. I (Chip) watched a roommate in college discover the power of infatuation.

When it all started, I was happy for him because he was shy and didn't have many relationships. I was surprised to hear him say, "Oh, Chip, she's just amazing. I've never been in love like this before."

About the tenth time he said some version of that statement, I asked, "So, what's her name? Is it somebody I know?"

He smiled, "Oh, I haven't actually met her yet. I'm still working up the courage to find out her name."

"Well, how do you know you're in love?" I asked.

He answered, "Man, when she walks across campus, you wouldn't believe the feelings I get just watching her."

I won't bore you with the details, but this went on for days. He eventually managed an introduction; then our conversation took on a new urgency. He would stand half-dressed in our dorm room, asking somewhat confused questions: "Chip, what do you think looks better, this shirt or that one? What about these shoes? I've got my basketball shoes—I could wear them. I might see her today."

Every time we talked, it was about how he was going to look, what kind of impression he was going to make. What

was his focus? Himself. I'm not saying that looking your best isn't important, but my roommate was missing the point.

A person in love thinks less about how he or she is going to look and feel in the relationship and more about what he or she can do to make the other person look and feel great. It's not all about you.

_____ **#4 An infatuated individual may be "in love" with two or more people at the same time.** True love is focused only on one person. Just after I (Chip) graduated from college, I was dating a girl still in school at another college. Most of what we had was infatuation. I didn't know her very well, but we were building a quasi-relationship. We weren't even seriously dating, but I was beginning to think that maybe she was "the one" because I was having these feelings.

Meanwhile, I ended up on a Christian basketball team that traveled all over South America. At our first stop in Puerto Rico, we played a good team in a big stadium. After the game I met this really nice girl who was a missionary there, and we ended up going on a very romantic picnic together. I can still remember the color of her dress. I also remember that I had feelings. I found myself attracted to her. My response caught me by surprise because the feelings were similar to those I was having toward "my girl at home."

Then we flew to Peru, where our missionary host had a daughter a year or two younger than me. She was cute in a "you just have to look twice" way. I fell instantly in love with her. Suddenly I couldn't remember what "my girl at home" looked like.

When we got to Santiago, Chile, we were welcomed with a huge dinner. I don't remember the food, but I do recall the girl who sat across from me with dark brown eyes, a sparkling smile, and beautiful, long, dark hair. Her laughter made up for the fact that I couldn't understand anything she said to me in Spanish. I did my own translations, believing that everything she said to me was highly complimentary of my skills and appearance. She never saw it, but I handed my heart across the table to her about halfway through the meal.

We visited five countries in a few weeks and I ended up in love with five different girls plus the girl from back home. Do you know what I learned? I learned that what I felt had practically nothing to do with love. It was all about chemicals. I could be attracted to a lot of different people, but that wasn't love. My infatuation switch was simply stuck in the "on" position.

_____ **#5 Genuine love creates a sense of security and feelings of trust. An infatuated person often feels jealous because he or she doesn't trust the other person.** Security grows and flows out of deep awareness of the other person's character, values, and track record. You know who they really are. And when you know who they really are, you trust them. You are not jealous because you know their heart is yours. Jealousy is often a sign of a lack of trust, and a lack of trust is a sign of infatuation.

_____ **#6 Someone who's infatuated loses his or her ambition and interests in everyday things and daydreams of unrealistic ideals that won't ever really happen. A person in love works hard to better him- or herself for the other person's benefit.** People in infatuation only think of their own misery. They often daydream of unrealistic objectives and ideals that neither person could ever actually attain.

Have you ever been around someone who's terminally infatuated? The things they used to be involved in—youth group, clubs, sports, whatever—seem to have been affected by their "love bug." They're suddenly living in la-la land. That's not love—that's brain damage.

If you're in a relationship and the other person is so glassy-eyed all the time that he or she can't get anything done, suspect infatuation. Infatuation feeds off the relationship; love builds into the relationship.

_____ **#7 A couple in love openly faces problems and tries to solve them. Infatuated people sweep problems**

the revolution: one + one

under the rug and try to pretend they don't exist. Have you ever had this scenario played out in real life?

You run into a friend at the mall whom you haven't seen since her family moved across town and she started going to a different church. She's holding some guy's hand and the two of them are walking into walls and the "You are here" mall signs because they can't take their eyes off each other.

She sees you and, after the customary squeal and hug, starts telling you about her guy. "We're in love," she says, as he wanders off to sample freebies from the food court. "We met yesterday (or last week or two weeks ago). God showed us we're meant to be together. It's just so amazing!"

"Wow," you say, both skeptical and curious. "How exactly did you two meet?"

"Well," she sighs. "I dropped my purse at the gas station and he picked it up and our eyes met. Then I found out that his last name starts with an *S*, and I had been praying for someone whose last name starts with *S*, so there—we know it's from God."

Before you can express your amazement, she babbles on, "What's so incredible is that even though he's not a Christian, he's just this really great guy. He's been out of high school a couple of years and he has a kid. I like kids. I graduate in June and we're hoping to get married then. God has made it so clear that he's the one. He doesn't have a job, but I know he'll find something soon. We're going to live with his parents until he can find steady work, and I'll stay home and take care of the baby. The baby's mom lives there too—something about a house arrest. I don't know the whole story, but I'm sure it will work out."

Okay, that's extreme. But if you're letting every warning sign smack you in the face and you still keep going, you're probably not in love—just infatuated. God wants us to love him with all our heart, soul, mind, and strength (see Mark 12:30). Don't you think that he would expect us to love each other the same way too? Love doesn't mean shutting down your brain, and it doesn't mean ignoring all the problems and warning signs. Instead, in love you face the challenges together and work through them together, seeking wisdom and strength from God.

_____ **#8 Love understands that giving someone space is a good thing. Infatuation imagines that love means intense closeness 24/7.** If circumstances require you to be separated from the one you love, that will teach you a lot about the quality of your relationship. If you've been going out for a while and you call each other three, four, or five times a day or you just have to see each other every day, that's not a good sign. That means you're trying to keep the feelings alive. If you both don't have lives and you don't have some away time, you probably have a lot more infatuation than love going on.

_____ **#9 Physical attraction is part of true love, but it only plays a minor role. It's the central focus of infatuation.** Physical attraction is an important part of relationships, but it's not the most important. We've been effectively brainwashed to believe that attraction is the surest test of whether or not we're in love. Actually, being attracted to someone doesn't mean that we are in love at all. It simply means that the person we're attracted to is good looking.

Don't read "small part" to mean "no part." If your heart doesn't skip a beat now and then and you don't feel real attraction to the object of your affection, that's a problem. But physical attraction takes a relatively smaller role when a couple is building a healthy relationship. It may be what captures someone's attention at first, but it's not what keeps him or her there long enough to develop a love relationship. Infatuation, however, makes physical attraction the sole test of love.

_____ **#10 A couple in love usually expresses physical affection later in a relationship. In infatuation, affection**

the revolution: one + one

is expressed earlier, sometimes in the very beginning. Maybe the first date starts out with a kiss, maybe more. But without the genuine love to back it up, affection ignites and consumes the relationship quickly. It makes you think the relationship is "close," but the closeness is artificial and fragile. When affection grows out of deep understanding and growing friendship, it gains in meaning and value.

_____ **#11 Love tends to endure. Infatuation may change suddenly and unpredictably.** Real love is stable. The best way to test stability in a new relationship comes through knowing that person in the context of his or her other relationships. How does he or she relate to parents, friends, and siblings? How stable are his or her relationships? Does he or she genuinely work at relationships, or use people? What's his or her track record? Is there a pattern that sets off any warning signals?

_____ **#12 A couple in love cares about when they're getting married, but they don't feel an irresistible drive toward it. Infatuated couples can't wait to tie the knot.** We see this one a lot with some Christians. They get to a point where they're not sure what they're going to do next (or they're just scared to take the next step), so they think marriage is the best solution. They meet someone and get in a huge rush to plan the wedding. Postponing it is out of the question.

What's up with that? Why wouldn't a couple wait and do it at the right time in the right way? Why wouldn't a couple want to deal with the real issues so they could have a solid marriage?

Love vs. infatuation—how did you do? Love takes effort, doesn't it? It takes time to get to know someone. If you want to love someone in a revolutionary way, you have to work at getting to know him or her. You have to live out the friendship. You have to respect the brother/sister boundaries. And you have to make his or her spiritual growth a top priority.

When you do those things, you show love. You show stability. And you are more sure about what you think and feel because you understand this person on a whole new level than just the butterflies in your stomach. Those feelings are great, but let's just call them what they are. They're not true love—those ooey-gooey feelings are pure infatuation.

Maybe you can see why so many marriages, even Christian marriages, end in divorce. When people think infatuation is love, they often make tragic, life-altering decisions with huge consequences. That's why God says, "Walk in love" (Ephesians 5:2 NASB), not feelings. And that's why sex180 is about getting God's best and not settling for anything less.

If you've lived out the revolution, even your breakups are going to look so different from your friends'.

"But what if the relationship doesn't work out? What if we break up?" If you do the relationship this revolutionary way, a breakup isn't going to devastate your life. You haven't crossed any physical boundaries. You have a friendship that's solid. And instead of walking away with a lot of baggage or scars, you walk away having grown spiritually. It may hurt. It may sting. You may be sad that the relationship didn't work out. But if you've lived out the revolution, even your breakups are going to look so different from your friends'. Your life will be enriched by others' lives, and you will have had the chance to enrich theirs as well.

In talking about her boyfriend, Krista said, "Even if we do break up and it does hurt, I'm going to grow through this. This is part of what makes me who I am. Having a boyfriend has taught me how to deal with people better. And I will grow and work through the breakup, if and when it happens."

So we've walked through the revolution of one.

We've seen what it looks like when you add one + one.

And that's all good, but there's a world out there dying that needs something revolutionary. They need a sex180. They need a second sexual revolution.

And they need you to bring it to them.

Even if you don't think you are part of the revolution, you are. You can do this.

It's time to launch a revolution.

the revolution:
one + the world

12

revolution gear

We have a confession to make: we love the Bible. That's probably not a huge surprise. After all, Chip is president of Walk Thru the Bible (not just a clever name), and Tim writes/edits a devotional magazine called *YouthWalk* that gets students into the Bible every day. To us, the Bible isn't just a fashion accessory for when we go to church; it's our daily source of life (along with coffee, another gift from God on a much smaller level).

But it wasn't always that way for me (Tim). I had to realize how much I needed it before I started reading it.

I've always had a Bible. I've always carried it with me to church, and it actually came in quite handy for keeping old bulletins, drawings, and notes I had written to my friends. But other than that, I never really flipped it open until somebody asked me to look something up in Sunday school or the pastor said, "Turn to . . ." My Bible was just another book on my shelf, and one I didn't like half as much as my comic books or some of my favorite novels.

The Bible isn't just a fashion accessory for when we go to church; it's our daily source of life.

I had always been the "good" Christian kid. I liked church, and it was where I found a lot of support and encouragement that seemed to be lacking at school and in my friendships. I prided myself on knowing all the right answers in Sunday school and my ability to "serve God" by singing solos or performing in drama productions. (Honestly, all I was serving was my insecurity.)

But when I transferred to an out-of-state college, my good boy facade started unraveling. I always knew I was sinful because that's what I had been told. I knew I made some mistakes, but I really thought I was basically a good person.

But then I got involved with someone sexually, and I came face-to-face with my sinfulness in a big way. A couple of people called me out on it, but I wasn't willing to walk away from the relationship. Finally, God orchestrated the end of the liaisons and I was left wondering, *What in the world did I just do?*

The shame of my sin was overwhelming. It's not that I had never had a sexually impure thought before then, but I had always told myself there was a line I wasn't going to cross.

I not only crossed it, but for a month I erased it.

And when I woke up, I was at rock bottom. Friendships started disintegrating. I was all alone. More lonely than I had ever been in my life (and I had been lonely lots of times). I had nowhere else to turn but to God.

So I opened my Bible. I still remember the passage of Scripture I read, 2 Timothy 4:16: "At my first defense, no one came to my support, but everyone deserted me. May it not be held against them." I had much bigger issues going on than my loneliness, but God cared enough to meet me there first. He showed me through his Word that I wasn't the only one who ever felt lonely or abandoned.

I saw myself in the Bible that day. I saw that somehow this book had something to say about what I was going through, and I wanted to know more.

the revolution: one + the world

That's when I fell in love with the Bible. I started reading it every day. I used the concordance in the back to look up all kinds of verses about loneliness. And as I looked stuff up, I began to learn about God, who he was and what he said about me. That's also when I really fell in love with God. It went beyond the words I said and moved into how I lived my life.

If you've grown up in the church, how many times have you heard someone say, "You need to read your Bible every day"? We're guessing about a million—okay, maybe a million and one.

But it probably wasn't just "Read your Bible." That statement is usually followed by a list of other things a "good" Christian is supposed to do daily—pray, serve others, lead others to Christ, live a pure life, avoid sin, and take care of the poor, sick, and widowed. And that's just the beginning, because you know when you go to church, there's going to be something new added to the list that you'd better start doing.

It's overwhelming. How are you going to fit all that in with the other things on your "to do" list—stuff like chores, homework, band, football, baseball, work, cheerleading, youth group, whatever? After a while, you start tuning it all out.

You may even be feeling overwhelmed right now as you read this book. You're wondering if you need to make up some kind of cheat sheet to help you start out as friends, treat the other person like a brother or sister, and make their spiritual growth a top priority. And how are you going to fit in all that inward character, outward modesty, and upward devotion stuff?

Living out this sex180 sounds like a lot of work, doesn't it?

What if you forget something? Do you have to start all over?

Does that mean you're kicked out of the revolution?

Before you get too worked up and we have to jolt you back to reality, stop, take a breath, and listen.

You can't do this.

"Uh, excuse me?" you may be thinking. "You mean to tell me that I've read 11 chapters in this book and you picked *now* to tell me that I can't do this? Seriously? Thanks for wasting my time."

You can't live out this sex180 on your own—not without some help. We know that. But most importantly, God knows that.

You can't live out this sex180 on your own—not without some help. We know that. But most importantly, God knows that. That's why he says, "This is my heart for relationships and sex, so I'm going to give you what you need to live it out."

The one who invented sex and relationships wants to help you do it all right. Cool, huh? It's kind of like Bill Gates offering to help you figure out your computer or Shakespeare tutoring you on writing poetry—only way better.

It's not a cool T-shirt or a bracelet or a ring.

This gear is much sweeter than that.

[the handoff]

Before God can hand off the gear you need to live out this sex180, he wants to establish one key thing: he wants a relationship with you before he wants you to start a revolution.

Relationships are a big priority to God—and a relationship with you is a big deal to him. We know, it's pretty bizarre to think that God, the Creator of the universe, wants to hang out with each one of us. He wants to walk through life with us. And he wants us to live out his commands so we can get the most out of life. Yeah, we don't always get it either, but isn't it really cool?

But God didn't just say he wanted a relationship with us; he backed up his desires. He sent his only Son, Jesus Christ, to come to earth and become both human and divine. (We don't quite understand this one either, but it still is very cool.)

the revolution: one + the world

Jesus walked the earth and experienced life, but with one huge difference—he didn't sin. And because of that, Jesus could become the sacrifice needed to die for our sins, to bridge the gap between sinful us and a holy God. Before then, God and sin couldn't be in the same room together. But because of what Jesus did, we can now enter into God's presence. The price for our sin has been paid once and for all.

So what does that have to do with you? It all begins with you realizing that you've got a problem—your sin. Despite your best efforts, you'll never be good enough, perfect enough, or loving enough. You're flawed to the core because of your sinful nature. That's not a slam against you, just a reality. We're all flawed; we're all sinful (see Romans 3:23).

It doesn't take very long to figure that out. Let's say you make a vow: "Okay, I'm not going to lose my temper in traffic anymore. I'm going to keep my cool." You do your best to make sure that doesn't happen. You learn how to count to ten when you start feeling your anger getting out of hand. You do breathing exercises to relieve your stress. You visualize a calmer you sitting in your car.

Then one morning your alarm clock doesn't go off and you wake up late for school. You find out that your little brother unplugged your clock to recharge his cell phone. You hop in the shower and discover that he also used all the hot water. You run out the door past the single pancake left on the plate. *This just keeps getting better*, you think sarcastically.

You have ten minutes to get to school. If you take the back way you can make it. You breathe a sigh of relief. It's going to happen. You're going to make it to school in time.

But then she pulls out in front of you—an elderly woman who can barely see over the steering wheel—and she's driving s - u - p - e - r   s - l - o - w. You try to pass her but there's no way around her car.

You lose it—big time. You start screaming and yelling, even letting fly a few words that you didn't know you knew. Your best attempts to be a good person just got detoured. You just can't be good enough 24/7. You need divine help.

"Okay, I'm a sinner. Now what?" you ask.

Next, you acknowledge that Jesus Christ did something about this sin problem. And honestly, he was the only one who could because, remember, he was (and is) God's Son. He lived a sinless life (the only one) and was killed on a cross. But he not only died, he rose from the dead. Jesus paid the price for your sins. He covered your debt, and because of that, he bridged the gap between you and God.

So you confess, "Jesus, I'm a sinner. And I need someone who can do something about this. I believe you're the Someone. In fact, I believe you're the Son of God. And your death and resurrection was for me. Please forgive me. Come into my life right now. Help me live this life your way. I surrender everything to you."

And the journey begins. You can now talk to God directly. You can have a relationship with him. You not only can say you love him but you are given power to actually follow his lead and live a life of love and purity.

The sinful patterns and sinful desires are still there—but we're no longer a slave to them. We have a choice. See, not only did Jesus pay for our sins, but now the Holy Spirit lives in us, helping us to become more like Christ by giving us the desire and the power to let Jesus live out his life in us. He actually takes up residence in us and becomes our constant companion and friend by means of the Holy Spirit (1 Corinthians 6:19). By his power he chisels away all the rotten, sinful, twisted parts of our lives where we're just used to doing our own thing.

We're an extreme makeover—although it's a lifelong process, not just seven days.

It's a constant process, and we're the ultimate renovation project. The Holy Spirit acts as the deposit to get the work started—God's pledge to not leave us like we are. He loves us too much to do that. The Bible describes it like this: "It

the revolution: one + the world

is God who makes both us and you stand firm in Christ. He anointed us, set his seal of ownership on us, and put his Spirit in our hearts as a deposit, guaranteeing what is to come" (2 Corinthians 1:21–22).

Jesus came to give us new life and a new way to live—with some divine, internal help. That helper is the Holy Spirit. Jesus said, "It is for your good that I am going away. Unless I go away, the Counselor will not come to you; but if I go, I will send him to you" (John 16:7).

The Holy Spirit is part of your gear to live out this revolution.

If you're a follower of Christ, the Holy Spirit lives within you and helps you live out the sex180.

[the Holy Spirit]

God knew you would need help following Jesus's example. He knew that you couldn't become like Jesus Christ on your own. So Jesus' sacrifice paved the way for the Holy Spirit to move in and renovate your life. If you're a follower of Christ, the Holy Spirit is the one who helps you live out not only Jesus's commands but also his heart. He's the one who lives within you and helps you live out the sex180.

When you're flipping channels and you see a talk show where the guest is surprised to find out his wife has been cheating on him and she's surprised to find out that he's doing the same, and as you're watching a thought pops in your head, *That is so wrong! Sex is too sacred and too serious to play around like that!*—that's the Holy Spirit. He reminds you of the truth God has taught you. Jesus said, "The Counselor, the Holy Spirit, whom the Father will send in my name, will teach you all things and remind you of everything I have said to you" (John 14:26).

When you're trying to take all this head knowledge about God and sexuality and really understand it in your heart, the

Holy Spirit helps you make that transition. "Who among men knows the thoughts of a man except the man's spirit within him? In the same way no one knows the thoughts of God except the Spirit of God" (1 Corinthians 2:11).

When your body is screaming for some kind of deeper connection with the object of your affection and you're struggling to say no, the Holy Spirit reminds you that there's another way. "Live by the Spirit, and you will not gratify the desires of the sinful nature" (Galatians 5:16).

When you're not even sure what that looks like, the Holy Spirit points out the escape route from sin. "God is faithful; he will not let you be tempted beyond what you can bear. But when you are tempted, he will also provide a way out so that you can stand up under it" (1 Corinthians 10:13).

God doesn't just sit back and watch as you try your best to live out his truth. Jesus paid way too high of a price for that kind of "hands off" attitude. His love is much too great for that. He never leaves—he's there with us every step of the way (see Matthew 28:20). And through the Holy Spirit, God gives us the gear not only to live out this sex180 but also to become more like Christ.

[the Bible]

We've already mentioned the other piece of gear with which God's equipped you to live in a revolutionary way—the Bible. Ever since that time in my life I (Tim) talked about at the beginning of this chapter, I've approached the Bible in a different way. Sure, some days I will read something and think "Huh?" but most of the time I never cease to learn something new about God or myself as I read his Word.

Some verses I've read a hundred times, but sometimes the hundred-and-first time I read them, those same verses speak to me in a whole new, deeper way.

the revolution: one + the world

That's the Holy Spirit speaking to me. He speaks to you too. When you read your Bible and a verse, chapter, or even word seems to jump out at you and connect with your heart, the Holy Spirit is teaching you some new truth about God. You see, these two pieces of revolution gear are interlinked. They work together.

It's what makes the Bible not just an ancient book but something that is both relevant and alive. Hebrews 4:12 says, "The word of God is living and active. Sharper than any double-edged sword, it penetrates even to dividing soul and spirit, joints and marrow; it judges the thoughts and attitudes of the heart."

When you don't know what to do, the Bible gives you direction. "Your word is a lamp to my feet and a light for my path" (Psalm 119:105).

When you want to live pure, seeing sex as sacred and serious, it helps you do it. "Direct my footsteps according to your word; let no sin rule over me" (Psalm 119:133).

When you wonder, "How can a young man keep his way pure?" the Bible gives you the answer: "By living according to your word. I seek you with all my heart; do not let me stray from your commands. I have hidden your word in my heart that I might not sin against you" (Psalm 119:9–11).

When others make you feel like an idiot for what you believe, you can read, "You are my refuge and shield; I have put my hope in your word" (Psalm 119:114).

When you're afraid to speak out, the Bible gives you the support you need to do it. "Lord, consider their threats and enable your servants to speak your word with great boldness" (Acts 4:29).

When you need strength to go on, the Bible has what you need. "Man does not live on bread alone, but on every word that comes from the mouth of God" (Matthew 4:4).

The Bible is your gear not only for the revolution but for life.

revolution gear

The Bible is your gear not only for the revolution but for life.

You can live out the sex180—with God's help. On your own, you're just spinning your wheels.

But you have a part to play too. You are the one who chooses to open your Bible—not because you're supposed to but because you can't wait to see what God has to say to you today.

You're the one who recognizes that while you may feel like you're all alone in the revolution, the Holy Spirit is your daily help in living in a way that's 180 degrees different from everyone else. Not just because you want to be different but because you don't want to settle for anything less than God's best.

Now that you've got your gear, you need a plan for how you're going live the revolution.

[sexual purity demands a game plan]

You can expect certain results if you do a sex180:

- If you stay sexually pure, then you can expect to have better sex in your marriage.
- If you stay sexually pure, then you can expect your relationships to add to your life, not take away from it.
- If you stay sexually pure, then you can expect to avoid sexually transmitted diseases that are destroying so many lives.
- If you stay sexually pure and look for a potential mate who lives by the same values, then you can expect that when you marry, you will remain faithful to each other.

These things are true, but if you stopped here, you would face a huge problem. You will fail if you walk into the world armed with only head knowledge about God's 180 way to approach love, sex, and relationships. When it comes to our

the revolution: one + the world

hormones, we don't usually make decisions based on head knowledge. You need much more than facts.

We humans are emotional beings who make some of our most important decisions based on impulses and peer pressure. Think for a moment about the thousands of people who know about the dangers of smoking, overeating, and drinking and driving but whose actions directly contradict their knowledge of the facts. This same principle applies in the way we handle our sexuality. Facts will not be enough to control our actions.

You need a game plan.

We're guessing that if you closed this book right now, within the next twenty-four hours you would suffer some major setbacks in trying to implement this 180 in your life, even if you are fully resolved to do so. Between your habits and our culture's traps, you're an easy target. Before the day is done, you may watch a football game or other sporting event that will include enough commercials with innuendos and messages to plant in your mind subliminal thoughts like, *If I only had this kind of beer, or this kind of car, or that kind of deodorant, gorgeous women would be falling at my feet.* Or, if you're a girl, *If I start using that shampoo or wearing that secret lingerie, some handsome hunk with gorgeous hair and bulging biceps will appear in my living room and announce, "Baby! Where have you been all my life? I need you!"*

You need a game plan so you not only know what you have for the journey (your gear) and where you're going (all the stuff you've read so far) but also how you're going to get there.

[the game plan]

step 1: develop convictions

The first step in living a sex180 is to develop convictions. Purity requires a personal commitment to the truth. The particular truth we're talking about is in Ephesians 5:2–4:

> Live a life of love, just as Christ loved us and gave himself up for us as a fragrant offering and sacrifice to God. But among you there must not be even a hint of sexual immorality, or of any kind of impurity, or of greed, because these are improper for God's holy people. Nor should there be obscenity, foolish talk or coarse joking, which are out of place, but rather thanksgiving.

That truth forbids sex of any kind that is outside of God's ordained design of one man and one woman within the marriage commitment. Say with your heart and mind, "I'm not going to go there mentally. I'm not going to go there in the way I talk or in the things I joke about. I'm not going to go there in my lifestyle." This makes it a personal commitment, a conviction that will affect your choices.

We don't mean intellectually agreeing with what the Bible says or what research has revealed. We don't mean adopting the beliefs of others you admire. We're talking about a personal conviction where you own a certain standard. From your heart, you say, "I am going to make a personal, purposeful commitment to live a life where my mind will be sexually pure, my speech will be sexually pure, and my actions will be sexually pure. I'm going to do it God's way, whether I'm in high school, college, single, or married."

When you close this book or turn on the television or go on your next date, how will your actions demonstrate what you really believe?

How does what you say you believe affect what you do with sexual urges?

In what ways do you demonstrate your convictions when you get on the Internet or walk by the convenience store and notice all those magazines?

What happens to your convictions when you flip on the television and some sensual scene comes on and you know it's the antithesis of everything you believe about godly love?

the revolution: one + the world

Do you get sucked in, or do you express your convictions with the remote? That kind of conviction says, "I'm going to switch the station immediately, not because someone else is watching but because I'm convinced that God loves me so much that he allowed Jesus to die on the cross to deliver me from self-destructive behavior. He cares for me so much that I'm going to do life this way. Not because of anyone or anything else. This is between God and me—no matter what responses or repercussions I get from others. I'm going to do life God's way." That's a conviction.

step 2: think about the "after"

The second step of God's game plan is to ponder the consequences of sexual sin. Ephesians 5:5–6 lists some heavy consequences. People who do life, relationships, and sexual activity outside the boundaries of God's way eventually will experience some dismal results. Pondering consequences can provoke a certain amount of fear, and that's okay. Fear can be a legitimate and healthy motivation for delayed gratification.

We need to ponder carefully the spiritual price tag of not doing life God's way when we are tempted to indulge in sexual fantasies or sexual behavior. We need to remember the feelings of guilt and shame that always follow sexual sin and what it does to our relationship with God. We must force ourselves to calculate the relational price tag of what sexual sin will do to the person we're involved with. You would be amazed at what a powerful deterrent imagining a lifetime with HIV/AIDS or genital herpes in exchange for a few moments of pleasure can be. Or consider the physical, emotional, and financial price tag of discovering your girlfriend is pregnant. Or imagine when your uncontrolled passion results in a broken relationship.

Thinking about the consequences has to be both vivid and honest. It has to remove any sense of confidence in ourselves and our ability to stay true to God's plan on our own. The Bible warns, "If you think you are standing strong, be careful, for you, too, may fall into the same sin" (1 Corinthians 10:12 NLT).

step 3: make pre-decisions

The third step of the game plan is to make pre-decisions. Advanced decision making is absolutely essential for sexual purity. Ephesians 5:8 tells us to walk as children of the light. Certain areas in our spiritual lives require us to "stand firm" and do battle (see Ephesians 6:10–17), but certain areas in our spiritual lives require us to flee instead.

Second Timothy 2:22 describes what fleeing means: "Run from anything that stimulates youthful lust. Follow anything that makes you want to do right. Pursue faith and love and peace, and enjoy the companionship of those who call on the Lord with pure hearts" (NLT). The idea here is to escape lust. It's not about being strong; it's about knowing when to retreat.

You and I are not strong enough for every temptation. No one is. The key to our response is to think ahead about what we will or won't do. Let me give you a few examples:

When dirty jokes start at school. "I think the biggest way that people know all these deep secrets in your life is by your talk," Mike says. "I look at my Christian friends and non-Christian friends, and a lot of them are joking about the same stuff—sex. I know there are a lot of times when I make a lot of sexual innuendo jokes. What comes out of your mouth is your character. What you say kind of forms and shapes who you are. I think the biggest way for us to start a sexual revolution is to watch what's coming out of our mouths. Are we representing what we're standing for in our talk? Even if it's little jokes." Decide ahead what you will and will not talk about—or listen to.

When something comes on TV that is offensive or suggestive. If a show is on and people start taking off their clothes and you feel yourself being drawn in, use the remote in your hand and *beep!* it's gone. Don't say, "Oh, this scene will be over in a minute. I'll just watch it until they get back to the main story." When it comes on, turn it off. A pre-decision.

The same principles apply to certain magazines, stores, and movies. Pre-deciding is not about being legalistic; it's about being honest and realistic about yourself and God's best for your life.

Here's the game we play: "Let's see, where's the line? Here's the blatant sin. How close can I get without falling in?" God doesn't put barriers and warning signs up so that we will try to live right next to them. He gives us these so we'll run the other way!

Don't just ask what other Christians are doing to determine what you will do. They could be way off. Determine, through prayer and reading the Bible, what God wants *you* to do.

Make a pre-decision about how far you will go with the opposite sex when you are dating. Make a pre-decision about where you will go on the date and what time you will take your date home. Make a pre-decision about what parties you will go to and when you're going to leave. Make a pre-decision about what you will do when you see certain magazines or movies.

> **Pre-deciding is not about being legalistic; it's about being honest and realistic about yourself and God's best for your life.**

step 4: get accountable

Asking others to help you keep your commitments to God will empower you to walk in ways that are pleasing to the Lord.

Identify two or three people who will boldly and regularly check with you about your commitments. People who share your passion for living like Jesus in every area of life. People who will not only call you out when they see you doing something that doesn't line up with God's Word but will do so in a loving, supportive way.

You need people who will put down their masks and get real with you. People who will share what's really going on inside them—where they're struggling and where they're surrendering.

It's also a good idea for guys to find a group of guys and girls to find a group of girls to hold you to your personal commitment to living a life of inward character, outward modesty, and upward devotion.

The Bible says, "Though one may be overpowered, two can defend themselves. A cord of three strands is not quickly broken" (Ecclesiastes 4:12). If you stumble in your efforts to live out God's call, that person or group of friends can pick you back up again. "If one falls down, his friend can help him up. But pity the man who falls and has no one to help him up!" (Ecclesiastes 4:10).

While the Bible and the Holy Spirit are major gear for the revolution, you need to plan ahead to make sure you have a flesh-and-blood person in your life who can physically walk beside you and say, "I'm going to help you live this out."

["God stuff"]

To make sure that all you've learned about God's 180 way to view sex and relationships doesn't just get parked in your head next to all the other "God stuff" that you know you're supposed to do, God gives you the gear to live out the revolution daily. He equips you to live out his best. This isn't self-help stuff; this is divine-help stuff.

That doesn't mean you kick back and don't play a part. You have choices. You have decisions. And to prepare for whatever challenges are going to come your way as you try to live out this 180, you'd better think ahead about what you're going to do. Develop your plan.

the revolution: one + the world

Isn't it amazing that the God who says, "Here's what you should do" about sex, love, and relationships is also the God who says, "I'll walk alongside you and equip you to live this out"?

Once again, God's heart for you is revealed—and it's for your best.

But God's not just about you. He loves the whole world, remember?

He wants you to play a part in making that known.

That's how the lasting revolutions take place.

[the revolution inside]

- As you go through your daily routine, how much are you aware of the role the Holy Spirit plays in your life?

- How does the Holy Spirit help you? Encourage you? Convict you?

- Other than opening the Bible at a study, Christian organization/club, or youth group, do you ever read the Bible on your own? Why or why not? (Note: if you have trouble getting into the Bible, a devotional like *YouthWalk* magazine could help you connect the dots between your life and God's Word. Check it out at www.youthwalk.org.)

- What can you do to make better use of the gear God's given you for this revolution?

- Do you have a plan for living out this 180—in a way that reflects your passion for God and purity?

- Develop your own game plan. Start with developing convictions. Write down your personal convictions about what you will watch and listen to, how far you will go and when, etc. Take some time right now to jot down your initial thoughts.

- Think through some of the relationships and scenarios in your life (when you're alone, when you're with someone of the opposite sex, etc.). What are some of the possible scenes that could play out and the consequences of each? Learn how to attach consequences to your actions—it will help you think twice about why you're doing what you're doing.
- Pre-decide how you would handle some of the situations mentioned in step 3 (page 186) of the game plan.
- Who are some of the people in your life who can hold you accountable?
- How honest are you with those people? How honest are they with you?
- How much of what they say is based on the Bible? How much is their own opinions? Make sure that the people in your life who are seeking to help you out are also seeking God.

one + the world

Wendy's[1] parents were always open to spiritual things—well, kind of. They weren't really open to Christianity, just a lot of other types of spirituality. So when Wendy became a Christian when she was 12, she faced a lot of questioning about her faith and learned to defend her beliefs well. In other words, she knew a lot about Christianity.

But there was one area of her life in which Wendy had a major disconnect with her beliefs—her sexuality.

Her parents were good, moral people, but they didn't really talk about sex very much. When they finally sat Wendy down for "the talk," Wendy's response was, "So what do you want to know?"

By the time she was in high school, Wendy had been sexually active for a while—even while attending church regularly. "I understood that I wasn't supposed to have sex before marriage," Wendy explains, "but nobody really talked about the subject at youth group."

A month after she started dating her high school boyfriend, they had sex. At first Wendy felt bad about what she had done. But she didn't stop. She thought she was in love with this guy, and she also liked the way sex felt. She had bought into the lies from TV and music—that sex was the ultimate way a person could experience and express true love.

After a year and a half of dating, Wendy and her high school boyfriend broke up and went their separate ways.

While in college, Wendy continued her dual life. She found a great church in her college town and was an active part of the college and career group. But she also got involved in another sexual relationship—this time with a guy who was older than her and recently separated from his wife.

People at Wendy's church found out about her living arrangements and decided to confront her about it. But when Wendy's "friends" from church approached her, they weren't very friendly. There was nothing loving about the way they talked to her. Their words were very condemning, judgmental, and harsh. And that was the last they said to her because after that confrontation, they cut off all communication with Wendy, giving her the silent treatment every time she came to church or any group functions.

Wendy felt overwhelmed with guilt and anger. She knew what she was doing was wrong, but she was angry and hurt at how she was being treated. Her world was spinning out of control. She was depressed and running away—not only from other Christians but also from God.

So when Chelsea became friends with Wendy, Wendy's expectations were pretty low. She knew as soon as Chelsea found out about her other life, she would be gone. Chelsea did find out, and amazingly, she didn't go anywhere. When they talked about what Wendy was doing, Chelsea was very compassionate and honest. And afterwards, Chelsea stayed around. She was a part of Wendy's life. She continued to be her friend—even though at the time Wendy's situation didn't change.

Through that relationship and Chelsea's genuine concern and love, Wendy was drawn back to Christ. Chelsea loved her like Jesus did. She didn't justify Wendy's behavior or condone it, but she loved her in spite of it. Years later, they are still friends.

the revolution: one + the world

In time Wendy made other friends who supported her renewed commitment to God. And as she began to do a 180 and started connecting every area of her life with her faith, the revolution in her also began to change her criteria for the kind of guys she dated. She knew she had to be the right person to attract the right kind of person. She said, "I knew I needed to be with somebody whose relationship with the Lord was more important than his relationship with me."

Chelsea saw Wendy the way Jesus saw her. She didn't condone her sin. She didn't support what Wendy was doing, but she supported her and loved her. And through that love, Wendy saw Jesus's love in a way that she had never seen before. To her it was revolutionary—and it forever changed her life.

God cares for the Wendys of the world. God weeps over their hurt, pain, and guilt. Psalm 34:18 says, "The LORD is close to the brokenhearted and saves those who are crushed in spirit." Psalm 147:3 echoes that by promising, "He heals the brokenhearted and binds up their wounds." Psalm 56:8 declares: "You keep track of all my sorrows. You have collected all my tears in your bottle" (NLT).

God not only cares but also wants to get through to the Wendys of the world. How does he do it? Through regular people like Chelsea—through people like us. Can you think of someone you know who's doing life all wrong and assumes that God really doesn't care?

Can you think of someone you know who's doing life all wrong and assumes that God really doesn't care?

[not the only one]

"God so loved the world that he gave his one and only Son, that whoever believes in him shall not perish but have eternal life" (John 3:16).

There's something in that verse that a lot of Christians miss: God loves you—but he also loves the world.

He not only wants you to have his best when it comes to love, sex, and relationships—he wants that for everyone. First Thessalonians 5:9 says, "God chose to save us through our Lord Jesus Christ, not to pour out his anger on us" (NLT).

You can take all that you've learned from this book and keep it to yourself. You can live out your own sex180 and let the rest of your school, family, and friends fend for themselves.

It's their choice, right? Maybe. But they may not even know they have a choice.

After all, the other way to live out your sexuality has a lot of voices. Plenty of people are proclaiming that message.

Yeah, you can walk away and let this only be a revolution of one—but you're going to have to ignore a lot.

Just look around you. What kind of debris do you see? That's why you need to speak out. The Bible says, "Be ready to speak up and tell anyone who asks why you're living the way you are, and always with the utmost courtesy" (1 Peter 3:15 Message).

You need to speak out with your life and the love of Christ to that guy who thinks the only way he can find someone to halfway care about him is to use every girl he dates.

You need to speak out with your life and the love of Christ to that girl who says she loves Jesus but whose outfit says she also likes everyone looking at her body.

You need to speak out to every guy who thinks that a relationship is all about him and he can say or do anything he wants as long as his needs get met.

You need to speak out to that girl who thinks that just because she's not the hottest girl at school she has to get the guys by giving them whatever they want.

> Be ready to speak up and tell anyone who asks why you're living the way you are, and always with the utmost courtesy.
>
> —1 Peter 3:15 Message

the revolution: one + the world

You need to speak out to the guy with STDs. The girl who has had an abortion.

You need to speak out to every person who has sold out who they really are because they just want to be sexy.

You can speak out to every family that's been torn apart by every twisted lie about sexuality—abuse, rape, molestation, affairs, pornography.

You speak out with your life, with your words, with genuine concern, and with love—real love. Not a "have to" love but a love that says, "I care too much to see you living a lie. I care too much to see you settling for so much less. I care too much to see you searching for something you're never going to find in those relationships."

Most of all, you want to speak out for God's heart. You've seen it. It's changed you. His love. His boundaries. His passion to give you his best. All things you can't walk away from because deep down, you know it's truth. It's what your soul was longing to hear.

It's what their souls are longing to hear too.

The world needs to hear. *Your* world needs to hear.

You're living it.

Now it's time to say it.

It's not about reciting a script.

It's not about reading off a page from this book.

It's not about judging or feeling superior to others.

It's about telling what God has done in your life, in your relationships, in your heart. It's about telling your story and how God has written this chapter.

You can do this. God's given you the gear.

You can change your world. You can launch a revolution in your house, in your school, at your part-time job, in your club, on your team, in your youth group.

God will provide the opportunity—you just have to do something with it.

Whether you like it or not, you're a revolutionary.

"Thanks but no thanks," you may be thinking. "That's not really who I am. I'm not really a leader."

But you are. In fact, every one of us is called to lead at some point in our lives. It's a matter of whether you're willing to step up and answer that call.

In his book *Summoned to Lead*, author Leonard Sweet says:

> We're all "players" in life. Yet sometimes life summons "players" to be "leaders." It may happen only once or twice in life. Sometimes life takes shape in such a way that a player is like the missing piece of a puzzle: the exact fit for the situation. Up to that point, the jagged pieces of your life don't seem to fit into any significant pattern. But then life calls you and summons you forth. A player in life becomes a leader, and even "born leaders" find themselves following the summoned leader.[2]

There's no such thing as a natural leader. Everyone has a moment (or moments) when they are called to lead.

There's no such thing as a natural leader. Sure, there may be someone who enjoys the spotlight more, has better organizational skills, or has a more persuasive personality than you—but everyone has a moment (or moments) when they are called to lead.

It's not always big things like a revolution. Maybe you're asked to lead a club at your school, lead a Bible study at your youth group, or lead your band.

When those moments come along, you can sit back and wait for someone else to do it, someone with a few more skills than you. But you may be waiting for a while.

Sometimes you just have to do something.

the revolution: one + the world

And whether you think you're the perfect person for the job isn't the issue. It's a matter of who will hear the call and obey. Besides, God chooses unusual people to lead others.

[isn't there someone else?]

When God appeared to Moses at the burning bush and told Moses that he would lead the Israelites out of Egyptian captivity, Moses's first reaction was, "Who, me? You've got to be kidding!" (not an exact translation, but pretty close—see Exodus 3–4). And he had a good point. After all, Moses was on the run. He had fled Egypt after murdering an Egyptian and had been hiding out in the desert ever since.

Maybe you can relate. Maybe your past history is less than stellar. You've made some mistakes. You've used people. You've had sex. You've never really connected your faith and this area of your life. So shouldn't God use someone a little more perfect—someone who has never made a mistake in this area? Maybe someone who wears a big *V* on their sweater and shouts their virginity not as a declaration of their purity but more as an "I'm so much better than you" attitude?

The irony is that God never calls the people who—in our culture or in the church—we would lift up on a pedestal and think is the perfect person for the job because, well, he or she is perfect (or at least appears that way on the outside).

If you look at most of the heroes in the Bible, like the ones mentioned in Hebrews 11, you'll see that for his various tasks God consistently picked those who had a few skills and a *lot* of brokenness. The people he wants serving him and carrying out the things that are close to his heart are the ones who realize that they don't have it all together and need God's help for the job.

For some reason Moses was the person God chose to go to Pharaoh and demand that the Israelites be released from their captivity. Moses didn't share God's confidence. In fact, he knew a lot of reasons why he wasn't the man for the job. Maybe they sound like yours.

[who do you think i am?]

Moses said, "Who am I, that I should go to Pharaoh and bring the Israelites out of Egypt?" (Exodus 3:11).

Moses thought he was the last person in the world who could convince Pharaoh to do anything. There had to be someone with a better reputation and better skills who could handle the job, right? Someone with a higher profile than a former palace resident/murderer/shepherd/fugitive from justice.

God knew Moses's resume, but God wasn't expecting Moses to pull off this task on his own. "I will be with you," he said (Exodus 3:12).

God's not expecting you to do this revolution alone. If you stand alone at your school or in your home or with your friends, you're never really alone. He's there with you.

[they're going to think i'm crazy]

Moses had another good point: "What if they do not believe me or listen to me and say, 'The LORD did not appear to you'?" (Exodus 4:1). Pharaoh might think Moses had spent a little too much time alone with his sheep or that he should have been wearing a little more sunblock to keep from frying his brain.

God told Moses to throw down his staff. Moses did, and it became a snake (Exodus 4:2–3).

God took something from Moses's life, something that was a part of his normal daily routine, and asked Moses to surrender it to God in obedience. Then God turned it into something holy. "This," said the Lord, "is so that they may believe that the LORD, the God of their fathers—the God of Abraham, the

the revolution: one + the world

God of Isaac and the God of Jacob—has appeared to you" (Exodus 4:5).

What's God asking you to give him? What is something from your life that when you hand it over to him, he can use for his plan—a position you hold, a group you're a part of, a skill you have, a friendship, a broken family? God gives you opportunities. He probably has already placed you exactly where he wants you to declare his truth. He's preparing you daily for the opportunity.

[this doesn't quite fit my skills and abilities]

Moses continued, "O Lord, I have never been eloquent, neither in the past nor since you have spoken to your servant. I am slow of speech and tongue" (Exodus 4:10).

God knows every strength and every weakness in your life. He knows what he's getting when he asks you to step up and lead. As he told Moses, "Who gave man his mouth? Who makes him deaf or mute? Who gives him sight or makes him blind? Is it not I, the LORD? Now go; I will help you speak and will teach you what to say" (Exodus 4:11–12).

[no thanks. i'll pass on this one. maybe next time.]

Moses asked God, "Please send someone else to do it" (Exodus 4:13). God sent Aaron, Moses's brother, to help. But Moses wasn't off the hook. God wanted Moses to be a part of this. He wanted Moses to lead. He provided some support so Moses wouldn't feel like he was flying solo, but ultimately God was using Moses to get his message across. God said, "You shall speak to [Aaron] and put words in his mouth; I will help both of you speak and will teach you what to do. He will speak to the people for you, and it will be as if he were your mouth and as if you were God to him" (Exodus 4:15–16).

Maybe you feel the same way Moses did—"God, I'll pass on this one. Let someone else take this on."

Maybe we could get by with that in the past. But it's not going to work anymore. Too many people are dying around you. And once you know the truth, you have to do something with it.

God will provide the moment for that to happen. You'll know because the Holy Spirit will make it so clear and obvious that if you decide to walk away, you'll know you have not only missed out but also disobeyed God. And the moment will haunt you.

Once you know the truth, you have to do something with it.

[nothing random]

If you have your eyes open, you'll see that nothing is random about our world. Everything has a design, a purpose, a plan. All the unconnected, seemingly sporadic things in our lives come together in "aha" moments when we realize that God was working something much bigger all along.

Esther, who was a Jew, was living in the king's palace as his wife when she got word that Haman, a noble in King Xerxes' court, had put the word out that all the Jews were to be annihilated. The news came from Mordecai, Esther's cousin who had been like a father to her since her parents' deaths.

Esther wasn't sure what to do. The only way she could stop what was going on was to go to the king in person and ask that he spare her people. The problem? Even a queen couldn't go into the king's presence without an invite.

Esther sent the following message to Mordecai: "All the king's officials and the people of the royal provinces know that for any man or woman who approaches the king in the inner court without being summoned the king has but one law: that he be put to death. The only exception to this is for the king to extend the gold scepter to him and spare his life.

the revolution: one + the world

But thirty days have passed since I was called to go to the king" (Esther 4:11).

Mordecai responded, "Do not think that because you are in the king's house you alone of all the Jews will escape. For if you remain silent at this time, relief and deliverance for the Jews will arise from another place, but you and your father's family will perish. And who knows but that you have come to a royal position for such a time as this?" (Esther 4:13–14).

Esther decided, "Okay, I'll do this, but I'm going to need some backup. I'm going to need some support." And she put out a request to make sure that it wasn't just her walking into the king's presence but that God was right there with her. She told Mordecai, "Go, gather together all the Jews who are in Susa, and fast for me. Do not eat or drink for three days, night or day. I and my maids will fast as you do. When this is done, I will go to the king, even though it is against the law. And if I perish, I perish" (Esther 4:16).

What's it going to take for you to speak up? At what point do you say, "I don't care about the obstacles that are in my way, I'm going to do this"?

Are you going to wait till it costs you something? What's the price going to be to motivate you? Your friends? Your family?

Or are you going to let the price others are paying be reason enough to speak out?

[speak out]

You don't have to be a super-alpha male/female who always wants to be in charge. You don't have to be the person who's always looking for a cause.

This revolution is for every person. Every type. Remember, God gives you opportunities. He places you in positions "for such a time as this" (Esther 4:14). You just have to seize them.

For Ella Gunderson, it happened at the mall.

Ella was shopping at a local Nordstrom department store in Washington with her older sister Robin and her mom. Her sister was trying to find the right pair of jeans, and Ella was just sitting on the floor outside the dressing room.

The sales clerk at the store encouraged Robin to buy the smaller size so she could have "the look"—tight and sexy. As her sister continued to shop, Ella was her normal, quiet, 11-year-old self. But on the inside, her mind was racing.

Ella was tired of there only being one way to look. She was tired of a culture that says, "This is how you have to dress if you want to be fashionable."

So when she got home, she decided to write a letter to Nordstrom. She was polite in her letter but very straightforward about what was on her mind.

"I see all of these girls who walk around with pants that show their belly button and underwear," she wrote. "Even at my age, I know that is not modest."

"With a pair of clothes from your store, I would walk around showing half of my body," Ella wrote. "Your clerks suggest that there is only one look. If that is true, then girls are supposed to walk around half-naked. I think that you should change that."

Ella didn't picket the store. She didn't organize a boycott. She didn't do something her mom or dad prompted her to do. In fact, they had no clue what was going on until Ella showed her mom the finished letter.

Ella mailed the letter, and what happened next was something none of her family really expected: someone read it. And not only did someone read it, but they wrote back. Kris Allan, store manager of Nordstrom Bellevue, and Loretta Soffe, vice president and central mer-

> **The sales clerk at the store encouraged Robin to buy the smaller size so she could have "the look"— tight and sexy.**

the revolution: one + the world

chandising manager for Nordstrom Brass Plum, wrote Ella individual letters thanking her and insuring her that her suggestions would be taken seriously.

But it went beyond that too, because word got out about Ella's letter, and she received national attention—including interviews on CNN and NBC's *Today* show. Not exactly what a shy 11-year-old girl intended. In fact, Ella doesn't think that being in the limelight is really making a difference. But she's willing to do what God wants her to do.

"We are glad to serve the Lord in whatever way He asks," Mrs. Gunderson said on behalf of her family. "He chose Ella, and when the Holy Spirit prompted her to write the letter, she said yes," she explained. "When He spurred the media to request interviews, she said yes. When He asked her to go way out of her comfort zone and appear on TV, she said yes."[3]

Ella was given an opportunity. God showed her something in her world that was broken, and when she decided to speak out, she became a revolutionary—a shy, 11-year-old revolutionary.

She didn't start grabbing clothes and tearing them apart. She didn't shout out to every girl who walked out of the dressing room in a barely there outfit, "You look like a whore!"

No, Ella wrote a letter. That may seem passive to some people, but it was huge for Ella. And look what happened.

> **Your clerks suggest that there is only one look. If that is true, then girls are supposed to walk around half-naked. I think that you should change that.**
>
> —Ella

[the revolution outside]

What about you?
Where has God placed you? What has he shown you?
It's time to step up.

Ella was given an opportunity. And when she decided to speak out, she became a revolutionary—a shy, 11-year-old revolutionary.

There are too many people dying—physically, spiritually, and emotionally—not to.

We're not going to take it anymore.

This is now a revolution of one + the world—for you and for them.

the revolution: one + the world

daily revolt

Every revolution starts somewhere! I (Chip) was teaching sex180 to about 3,500 to 4,000 teens and young adults in Atlanta about a year ago. They heard what you've been reading in the last 13 chapters. The place was packed, the music had been awesome, and you could hear a pin drop. So I called out the question, "Will you step up and step out to launch a second sexual revolution in your school, among your friends, and in your relationships?"

With everyone watching, I asked who would stand up and proclaim their commitment to be a radical revolutionary for the glory of God.

About 300 to 400 students stood up, while thousands of others sat in their fear and indifference. It wasn't a huge, hyped-up thing. It was a small group of people who rose to their feet because they wanted to, not because they felt like they had to. They had a passion in them not only to live out the sex180 themselves but also to reach out to people around them.

Some banded together in small groups immediately after we ended and devised a strategy to launch a revolution in their high school. The students you've heard from in this book were part of that group. They have been revolutionaries for the past year in their large public high school.

So how about you? Are you a part of the second sexual revolution?

Has it started with you—the revolution of one?

Have you begun to see sex as both sacred and serious and then let that truth latch on to both your brain and your heart?

Are you a part of the second sexual revolution?

If you have, then now you can't turn on the TV, listen to your MP3s, go online, or watch a movie without the words "sex is sacred" and "sex is serious" whispering in your ear. You just can't see the world in the same way. Things that didn't used to be a big deal to you suddenly are, and the reason is that you are tuned into God's heart. There's no going back. Anything less is just lying to yourself.

But now you need to take it to the next level. You've got to let those beliefs affect other areas of your life too. You have to decide that instead of becoming a pawn of our culture, you are going to be a person who has inward character, outward modesty, and upward devotion.

If you do, you will not only think differently, you will act differently. Your life will be a sex180.

Those actions will be put to the test, and you'll be forced to decide if you are going to buy into the biggest lie of all—that your faith and your life don't have to connect, that you can keep all of that separate. You'll realize that not only do you need to do a 180 on what you think about sex, but the way you view relationships needs to change too. It's not just about knowing something, it's living it out. And if you are going to live out what God is doing in your life, something drastic has to change.

And so the revolution expands—one + one. That means you have crossed the line and become a part of God's solution by loving others in a way that transforms their lives.

the revolution: one + the world

You say, "I'm not going to play that way anymore" and say good-bye to the Hollywood way of doing relationships, a way that leaves a lot of carnage and scars.

You say, "I'm going to start out as friends. I'm going to see the other person as my brother or sister. And I'm going to make the spiritual growth of that person my top priority."

Love? You learn what it really looks like, and it's nothing like infatuation.

Breakups? Not so brutal.

People who used to know you may not even recognize you.

They will ask you questions. They will want to know why you do what you do.

People will see that you start out relationships different than they do.

People will see that you treat people with respect and dignity. That you just seem to know a lot more about those around you—important stuff like who they really are, what they believe, what and who they really care about—than other people do.

People will notice that the way you leave a relationship is so much different than the drama they go through.

People will notice that the things that are attractive about you have nothing to do with a skin-tight T-shirt, short skirt, or bare midriff.

People will see something different about your life.

So what are you going to do when they start asking you questions?

They will, you know. They're going to want to know your secret. They're going to want to know "why." Answers like "wait" or "no" aren't going to be good enough.

That's when you tell them about sex180. Not in a way that looks down on people. Not in a way that's preachy or arrogant. Not being self-righteous or thinking you're holier than everybody else. You know what we mean—the whole unspoken "we're Christians, you're not, we're smart, you're stupid" vibe we give off sometimes.

But when you love authentically and live pure, your life will shine. You can live in a way that impacts your friends, your own family, other students, your coach, whoever. And when you live it out first, your talk just attaches words to what people have already seen.

It doesn't matter that you're still a student—in fact, that probably gives you an advantage. The first sexual revolution was started by teens and young adults. You've got God backing you up on this one. First Timothy 4:12 says: "Don't let anyone think less of you because you are young. Be an example to all believers in what you teach, in the way you live, in your love, your faith, and your purity" (NLT).

When you love authentically and live pure, your life will shine.

Remember my (Chip's) free meal in West Virginia? I received a lot more than a home-cooked dinner that night. Not because Dave and Lanny, the couple I visited, wanted to preach a sermon to me. They didn't invite me there to straighten me out. But because of the abundance of love that filled their house, I saw what I had been looking for. It was so simple that I probably would have overlooked it if I had just seen them at church. But because they invited me into their lives, I got to see it up close.

They were just living their lives. They had no set agenda, other than wanting to feed a hungry college student. But when they shared a meal and their home, the light of their lives showed me a different way to live out my sexuality. I did a 180 that night.

Anything they would have said about sex or relationships would have been just backup for what I saw—a real relationship, a real love, and something worth waiting for.

I finally got it. I understood God's heart. Then I started living it out.

But first I saw it lived out.

That's why most of this book has been about how you live this out. Nobody's going to listen to what you say until they know you believe and see you live it out first.

Your life is shining "like stars in the universe as you hold out the word of life" (Philippians 2:15–16). The revolution begins in you.

Then it moves to one + one. Your relationships work better, and people want to know why. Now they're ready to listen.

"When it's time to talk, you'll know," Bobby says. "When they question, that's when you talk. You don't force it on anyone. You live it, and when they ask you about it, you go for it. What you do and how you live is what they see."

What do you say? You tell them about your own experience. You tell them why you do what you do and how that's working for you.

You get honest with them. If your past is less than stellar, you let them see that so they realize it's not just an already "perfect" person who can live this out—anyone can.

"I think a big way we can impact other people is not just to share with our friends, 'Don't have sex'—they've heard that many times before," says Mike. "I think people listen to the Christian who is honest and says, 'I've been through that situation.' Or 'I've been pressured by that.' I think the biggest way to impact other people is when they can relate to you. I think so many times we as Christians make it seem like we're the perfect people."

If you're tuned in enough to your walk with God to live out this revolution, you know very well how imperfect you can be at times. And because of that, you may be afraid to speak out about this sex180. You don't want to be a hypocrite. We don't want to be hypocrites either.

That's why you've got to be honest about your struggles. But when you fall, you don't run away from God—you run to him. Instead of letting the pain of your sin cause you to pull back, let it push you forward.

When you sin, confess it to God. First John 1:9 says: "If we confess our sins, he is faithful and just and will forgive us our sins and purify us from all unrighteousness."

After you confess it, God says he'll choose to forget. Then, instead of letting your sin haunt you, learn from your bad decisions. Look at what got you there and then move on, a little wiser. You may bear some scars. You may have to live with some of the consequences of your actions. That's just the nature of sexual sin. It leaves some long-lasting wounds on your brain and heart and sometimes body—part of the sacredness and seriousness of sex.

But it's not just about damage control. It's not about you saving face.

Remember, what was revolutionary about Jesus was his love.

Living out this revolution and telling others about it has nothing to do with people seeing how great or how pure you are—it's about seeing how awesome and loving God is. How he created sex. And how he desires to give it to you—with the right person at the right time in the right place.

Remember, what was revolutionary about Jesus was his love. Not because he led an army. Not because he took over the culture. But because when people had an encounter with him, they walked away with a new realization of God's love.

Plenty of belief systems say "no sex till marriage." But what makes this 180 different is the fact that it's backed up not by rules but by God's love. That's what people at your school need to hear.

"At the beginning of the year, our group was like, 'Let's go impact the school. Let's talk to everyone you know about God.' But that didn't work for me," Audrey admits. "I actually think I turned a lot of people away. The greatest commandment is love. The greatest commandment is not telling people what to do. Once you love someone, that's when you can make an impact. I've built some friendships this year, and because of

the revolution: one + the world

that I can tell them how I feel about stuff. It's a natural thing. It's God's plan. It's not me looking for an opportunity where it's not supposed to be."

If you don't know someone who needs to hear, ask God to lead you to someone. "I'm praying for God to open doors," Annie confesses. "I'm praying, 'Father, I'm living for you. I'm standing. I'm standing in your victory. I am ready to do whatever.' And out of the love of just friendships, God opens the door. It's so effortless."

[the revolution inside]

God's given you the gear to live out the revolution of one.

He's given you the plan to live out the revolution of one + one.

And he's given you the heart and the opportunities to live out the revolution of one + the world.

Revolt every day.

Live in a way that goes 180 degrees opposite from our culture.

Live out the sex180, and let's go start a second sexual revolution.

worldwide revolution

Can you change the world?

It's been done before. The revolutionaries in the first sexual revolution did it. They saw the hypocrisy in the culture and called it out. They saw people saying one thing and living another. They challenged the established values and thinking and even the ways their lives were manipulated. They made themselves and their views visible. They were willing to take on the status quo. They were brave. They were passionate.

What are you going to do with what you know?

And they changed the world.

Not always for the better, but they changed the world.

Now it's your turn.

What are you going to do with what you know?

You've seen the lies. You've seen the hypocrisy of a culture that says sex is just physical, that you can do whatever you want with whoever you want to do it with and it shouldn't be a big deal. It *is* a big deal. You can't separate sex that way—it's spiritual, emotional, physical.

You've watched your friends get to middle school or high school and suddenly act like the most important thing in their lives is to make sure everyone knows how they've changed physically. Everything else about them just isn't as important anymore.

You've seen parents, siblings, cousins, aunts, and uncles discard relationships and people because they were chasing after the right person instead of becoming the right person.

We've been played long enough. The manipulation is over.

We're going to live a different way, a 180 way, and when people ask, we're going to seize the opportunity to shout it. We're not going to let jewelry, a T-shirt, or a rally say it for us.

We're going to speak it first with our lives.

We're going to show that sex is sacred and serious by how we live. We're going to become people of inward character, outward modesty, and upward devotion.

When someone asks why, we're not going to throw out regurgitated answers. We own the answers—they're inscribed on our hearts. We know what to say not because it's what we were told but because it's what we believe.

We value God, people, and our sexuality too much to settle for anything less than God's best plan.

"It's important to see human worth the way God does," Audrey says. "God sees each of us and loves us individually. You have to see people as worthy of your time, effort, and love."

When we want others to notice us, we put on integrity instead of a tight shirt. When we want others to be attracted to us, we don't use our bodies—we live out our faith.

We're going to do relationships in ways that quit using and manipulating people. We're no longer going to leave a trail of debris behind us. We're going to stop living with regrets. Relationships are no longer about us—what we can get from the other person emotionally and physically. They're going to be about what we can give to someone else—spiritually.

We're going to quit paying the price the culture demands. It has already cost us so much.

the revolution: one + the world

Whatever we do, we're going to honor and reflect what God's doing on the inside of us.

We're going to use the gear God gives us to live out the revolution. And through that gear, we're going to be constantly reminded of his heart.

We're going to decide ahead of time how we're going to deal with whatever life throws at us. That includes what we do when we're alone in our rooms, online, with our crush, and with our friends.

This next revolution is going to look different for each of you—because your lives are different. You know your world, your friends, your family, your school better than anyone else. God has placed you there for a reason, a purpose, a time like this. He will give you the opportunities. When they come, don't wait for someone else to do something. Step up. Say something. Do something.

When opportunities come, don't wait for someone else to do something. Step up. Say something. Do something.

For Bobby and his girlfriend, one of those opportunities was at their school's homecoming dance. He said, "We looked around and saw all these people, even Christians we knew, doing this back-to-front dance. We were like, 'Whoa, what's going on?' We had this agreement that we weren't going to dance that way. So we grabbed hands and started dancing like third graders. It didn't matter. We had fun with it. We enjoyed it. At the same time, we were examples. You can't blend in with the crowd."

Quit relying on a T-shirt, book, CD, or pastor to tell the truth for you. People need to hear it from you. "Build the trust and loving friendship first," Bo says. "They'll figure out that if you love them and care for them and trust them that much, then they need to trust you're making the right choice. If they know you love them that much, then you can encourage them to make the right choice too."

What about you? What's it going to look like in your life? It's time to step up.

Walk out of the movie.

Move your computer into the living room.

Speak up to a friend you see letting the physical become the foundation of her relationship.

Plan what you can do to help your bf/gf grow spiritually, not just how "romantic" you can make your dates.

Shout out sex180 in your school newspaper.

Declare it in chat rooms.

Upload it online.

Talk about the "why"—and never, ever rely on the easy "wait" and "no" responses.

You'll know what you need to do.

Live out this sex180—and help others live it out too.

Dr. Martin Luther King Jr. said, "Freedom is never voluntarily given by the oppressor; it must be demanded by the oppressed."[1] We're demanding it. But not in a militant or obnoxious way.

This isn't about politics or power. This isn't a fad or a trend.

It's about living it out every day of our lives.

It's about doing life in such a way that makes it 180 degrees different.

It's about loving God and loving people.

That's truly revolutionary.

Welcome to the revolution.

> **Freedom is never voluntarily given by the oppressor; it must be demanded by the oppressed.**
>
> —Dr. Martin Luther King Jr.

the revolution: one + the world

notes

chapter 2: sex180

1. MSNBC News, "Nearly 3 in 10 Young Teens 'Sexually Active,'" January 18, 2005, http://www.msnbc.msn.com/id/6839072/.

2. Cynthia Dailard, "Understanding 'Abstinence': Implications for Individuals, Programs and Policies," *The Guttmacher Report on Public Policy* 6, no. 5 (December 2003): 4–6.

3. Jennifer M. Parker, "The Sex Lives of Christian Teens," *Christian Reader*, March/April 2003, www.christianitytoday.com/tc/2003/002/7.28.html.

4. Sarah St. John, "The Big V: Various Reasons Support Celibacy," Truman State University Index, April 3, 2003, www.trumanindex.com/news/2003/04/03/Trulife.

5. Les and Leslie Parrott, *Relationships* (Grand Rapids: Zondervan, 1998), 131.

6. Michelle Tauber, Thomas Fields-Meyer, and Kyle Smith, "Young Teens and Sex," *People*, January 31, 2005, 86–96.

7. Jim Hancock and Kara Eckmann Powell, *What (Almost) Nobody Will Tell You About Sex* (El Cajon, CA: Youth Specialties, 2001), 10, 56. Reprinted with permission from Youth Specialties, Inc.

8. Paula Reinhart, "Losing Our Promiscuity," *Christianity Today*, July 10, 2000, 32–33.

9. Hancock and Powell, *What (Almost) Nobody Will Tell You About Sex*, 10, 56. Reprinted with permission from Youth Specialies, Inc.

chapter 3: over it!

1. One Life Revolution, "Unbelievable Stats," http://domino-201.worldvision.org/worldvision/appeals.nsf/stable/olr_understand_stats_page1.

2. Philip Yancey, "Cry, the Beloved Continent," *Christianity Today*, March 2004, http://www.christianitytoday.com/ct/2004/003/28.112.html.

3. Family Safe Media, "Pornography Statistics," http://www.familysafemedia.com/pornography_statistics.html.

4. Janet Root, Compassion International, "The Millstone Report: Sexual Exploitation," http://www.compassion.com/resources/childpoverty/reports/default.htm.

5. Family Safe Media, "Pornography Statistics."

6. Ramona Richards, "Dirty Little Secret," *Today's Christian Woman*, September/October 2003, www.christianitytoday.com/tcw/2003/005/5.58.html.

chapter 6: extreme makeover: inside edition

1. Laura Sessions Stepp, "Nothing to Wear," *Washington Post*, June 3, 2002, C01.

2. Ibid.

chapter 7: relationships180

1. Parrott, *Relationships*, 134.

chapter 8: real friends, real benefits

1. Benoit Denizet-Lewis, "Friends, Friends with Benefits and the Benefits of the Local Mall," *New York Times*, May 30, 2004, final, sect. 6, 30.

chapter 11: what abouts

1. The twelve tests presented in this chapter are adapted from Henry Bowman, *Marriage for Moderns* (New York: McGraw-Hill, 1954).

chapter 13: one + the world

1. Wendy's name has been changed at her request.

2. Leonard Sweet, *Summoned to Lead* (Grand Rapids: Zondervan, 2004), 13.

3. The paragraphs in this section are adapted from and include direct quotations from the following article: Rebecca Grace, "Activism: Letter from 11-Year-Old Gets Attention of Retailer, Media," *American Family Association Journal* 28, no. 11 (November–December 2004): 11. Reprinted with permission.

chapter 15: worldwide revolution

1. Dr. Martin Luther King Jr., "Letter from Birmingham Jail," *Why We Can't Wait* (New York: Harper and Row, 1964); quotation found at www.brainyquote.com/quotes/authors/m/martin_luther_king_jr.html.

notes

Chip Ingram is president and CEO of Walk Thru the Bible and teaching pastor of *Living on the Edge,* Walk Thru the Bible's international broadcast ministry. Chip's passion is to partner with the local church to be a worldwide catalyst for discipleship. A graduate of Dallas Theological Seminary, he is the author of six books, including: *I Am with You Always*; *Love, Sex, and Lasting Relationships*; and *God: As He Longs for You to See Him*. Chip is also lead teaching pastor at The Bridge Church Atlanta. He and his wife, Theresa, have four grown children and three grandchildren.

Tim Walker is senior editor of *YouthWalk* magazine, a monthly students devotional magazine published by Walk Thru the Bible. He has also written ten articles for the online magazine *Relevant* and the award-winning devotional magazine *inDeed*. He is a graduate of Lee University in Cleveland, Tennessee, and lives with his wife and three sons in Woodstock, Georgia.

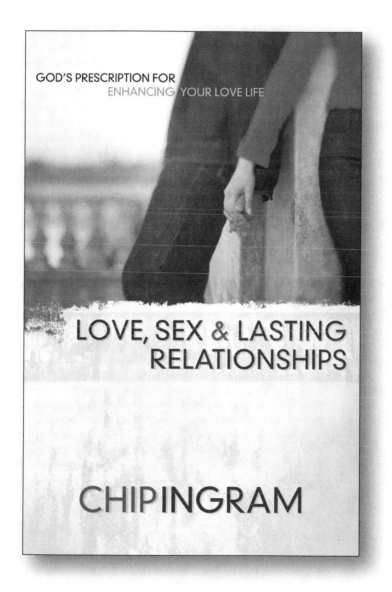

change you.
change your world.
YOUTHWALK.
gear for the revolution.

www.youthwalk.org
real life. real answers. real God.
a devotional magazine for students.
800-877-5539